Henrietta's Dream

Henrietta Spink

Henrietta's Dream

*A mother's remarkable story of love,
courage and hope against impossible odds*

Hodder & Stoughton

For my darling husband Michael and my wonderful sons Henry and Freddie

And Professor James H. Fallon – thank you for believing in my dream

Acknowledgements

I would like to acknowledge the help and support given by my compassionate and dynamic agent Kay McCauley; Cassandra Jardine, a great friend who prodded me into writing the book; Caro Handley, my editor, who gave me the gift of confidence; my publisher, Rowena Webb, who made it all happen so smoothly and, finally, all the team at Hodder.

There are only two ways to live your life. One is as though nothing is a miracle. The other is as though everything is.

Albert Einstein

Introduction

This is a book about an extraordinary journey. It's a journey I can sometimes hardly believe has been mine – a roller-coaster ride of incredible challenges, heartbreaking lows and dizzying highs. A journey which has taken me through my worst nightmares to moments of unbelievable happiness and back again.

We are an ordinary family. I grew up as the middle one of three sisters, got married to a lovely man and looked forward to bringing up children. My husband, Michael, and I expected to have a quietish life. A peaceful, ordinary life, with the usual share of ups and downs. We pictured ourselves with a fire in the grate, a vase of flowers on the table, classical music playing in the background and a couple of children playing happily at our knees.

That isn't what we got. The quiet life was clearly never going to be an option for us. What arrived instead was a life I'd never in my wildest dreams imagined. A life in which we were catapulted into the extraordinary and in which we found ourselves standing up to be counted, battling with bureaucratic giants, reading about ourselves in the papers, rubbing shoulders with celebrities one minute and on our knees with exhaustion and despair the next.

Our life with Henry and Freddie has confronted every preconception we ever had. Much of it has been an endurance test, stretching us to the limits of our patience, willpower and faith. We've had to examine our own beliefs and values, and we've come up against the best and the worst of other people's. Very little has run smoothly. I've had more moments of doubt and despair than I can count, and more knocks than has seemed fair or possible. I've had to fight every inch of the way for the care and facilities the boys needed, and to stand up and shout at times when I'd rather have crawled quietly into the nearest hole. There have been many moments of pain and hopelessness which have threatened to overwhelm me. As a result I've learned to spot the opportunity in every setback and the gift in every problem. And I've learned not to be afraid to stand up and make a noise and to challenge everything. I can truly say that my children have made me a warrior!

When my sons were born the dreams I had for them flew out of the window. In time I learned to live with a different set of dreams. Just because your children are disabled doesn't mean that you have no dreams for them. You dream as much as, perhaps more than, any other parent. I dreamed of seeing my boys, healthy and well, as laughing young men out in the world, able to lead their own lives. My dreams were usually dismissed by others as the pipe-dreams of a wishful-thinking mother. But those dreams have been what kept me going when all else failed.

If I'd been given the choice at the beginning, would I have taken this journey on? Probably not. But I wasn't given the choice. Instead I was given two extraordinary, marvellous and unique sons who would teach me that dreams, however outrageous, impossible and far-fetched, can and do come true. When you have handicapped children you ask yourself, 'Why me? What did I do wrong?' But you learn to fight self-reproach and pessimism, just as you learn to fight doctors who write your kids off and politicians who think doing something for the disabled will never be a vote-winner.

This book is not a manual on how to live with disabled kids. It's about facing life's challenges and believing that mountains can be moved. It doesn't matter what your wake-up call is. Mine happened to be two disabled children. What matters is the way you respond when it comes. You can sit on the fence and do nothing, but all you'll get is a sore bum. Or you can take your challenges in both arms, thank them for the lessons they bring, and live your life with passion, determination, courage and humour.

This book is about the journey my two boys have taken me on and the wonderful and amazing things I have learned along the way. Most of all, it's about the power of hope and the strength of dreams.

Chapter 1

_____

I found out that I was pregnant on a sunny day in early June 1987. I'd bought one of those pregnancy kits with a little plastic strip you have to pee on before waiting to see if it turns blue. Watching it slowly change was magical – I thought my heart would burst with joy. It felt like a moment of pure creativity, something beyond my control and utterly awe-inspiring.

I'd started throwing up almost as soon as we reached Bali the day after our wedding, and spent most of the next two weeks craving baked beans and very little else. So much for romantic Indonesian island dinners.

The minute we got back to our little house in Battersea in south London I had raced round to the chemist to get the pregnancy testing kit. When it proved positive Michael was as thrilled as I was. We were incredibly happy and just a little overwhelmed by the enormity of it all. Instantly we made plans. We both felt instinctively that it was a boy, though we would have been equally happy with a girl. We talked about schools and even looked at a few of the kind where you put your child's name down at birth to guarantee a place. I remember walking into a little school in Kensington just as the infant boys and girls were lining up for lunch. I looked down at my small bump and felt exquisitely happy.

Ours had been a whirlwind romance followed by a wedding beset by complications courtesy of my distinctly eccentric family. After months of pre-wedding chaos, altered plans and last-minute hitches we revelled in the post-wedding calm of life in our small terraced house.

Michael and I had met in May 1986. It was a chance meeting with an old family friend which led to the dinner party at which I was introduced to him. The friend was a man I'd last met in Malta, when I was ten years old and staying with my grandparents. Christopher had been a student then, and he and his friend David had driven my sister and me around the island. Now married, he invited me to dinner as a potential match for David, who was still unmarried. Michael was also at that dinner party. An art dealer, he'd just written his first catalogue and he'd been celebrating all day, with the result that he turned up more than a little tipsy. Friends had tried to sober him up by feeding him toast and Marmite before he came out, but their efforts had clearly been in vain.

Despite his rather inebriated state I found Michael engaging and entertaining and when he offered to drive me home I accepted, though when he asked to come in I said no and shut the door firmly in his face.

Three days later I bumped into him at another party. He was considerably more sober this time, though still just as entertaining. Once again he drove me home, and once again I refused to invite him in.

The next day he phoned. I was in the bath and told my ten-year-old sister Tilly to get rid of him. She asked him to ring back in twenty minutes. Hideous child. With some reservations, I agreed to a date. Much as I liked

Michael, I wasn't sure I was ready for another relationship. It had only been a year or so since I'd left my previous boyfriend, and I was still reluctant to get involved again.

At the age of seventeen I had run off to stay with a girlfriend of mine who was studying at the Sorbonne in Paris. We bought Inter-rail tickets and decided to go on a tour of Spain and Morocco, where we fell in with a group of Spaniards who offered to drive us around. By the end of the month I had fallen for one of them, Pedro. I was pretty aimless in those days, having left school with a handful of O-levels and not much idea of what to do next. I'd trained as a bookbinder, at which I had excelled, finishing the year-long course with a distinction and winning a national competition for classical binding. However, I had no idea how to set up a business or what I should do next, so hitching up with this Spaniard was an easy option. He was a complete lunatic who had spent some time in the French Foreign Legion. He turned out to be incredibly manipulative and it had taken me several years to liberate myself from him.

I came back to England and found a job as a book conservator with the National Trust for a year. This gave me the courage to set up my own bookbinding studio, and I felt at last I was in control of my life again. Around this time I was introduced by another client to David Khalili, a rich Iranian dealer in Islamic art in Bond Street. I'd just seen the most wonderful Islamic art exhibition at the Victoria and Albert Museum, so this meeting was like coming home. I went to work as a freelance for David, specialising in Islamic book and manuscript restoration.

I was thoroughly enjoying myself being totally independent, but over drinks and dinner with Michael I began to fall for him. He couldn't have been more of a contrast to my previous boyfriend. He was bright, articulate and happy, with a huge beam of a smile and eyes that laughed all the time. He'd been to Cambridge and had left with a good degree in history, despite the fact that boozing, girls, punting on the river and getting up after noon had generally taken priority over his studies. After graduating he joined Spink and Son, the firm of art dealers his family had founded four hundred years earlier. He had always wanted to work there and loved it from the start. His cousin was chairman, and he and Michael were the last two Spinks to work in the family firm – only a few years later it was taken over by a major auction house.

Eleven days after our first meeting Michael took me to Paris for the weekend. We stayed in a sleazy little hotel on the Left Bank where he had stayed before. A very French *concierge* eyed me up and down as we arrived, clearly viewing me as another floozie in a long line of girlfriends. Michael wasn't the slightest bit abashed.

That lunchtime we climbed the steps of Montmartre to the Sacré Coeur, leaving the drone of Paris below us. We sat at a café in the square nearby, drinking and watching the world go by. It was an exquisite, sunny day and the smell of ground coffee and freshly baked bread hung in the air, while pigeons scoured the ground for crumbs, children chased one another and artists enticed passersby to sit for portraits. I looked down and there on the crisp, white tablecloth was a little leather box. Time stood still. I looked up to find Michael grinning. He proposed very traditionally and I said yes. I knew with absolute surety that I wanted to marry this lovely man.

I felt so elated and proud, as though my life had just begun. I wanted to tell the whole world. That weekend was probably the most romantic of my life. Michael and I both felt so sure that this was right: we had liked one another instantly, become best friends, had so much in common and our relationship felt very straightforward and easy. We just loved being together. When we came home we met each other's families. I adored Michael's from the start. His father, Farley, and mother, Lamorna, lived in a large, rose-covered house in Surrey. His father was a GP who went on to specialise in homeopathy, while his mother was a physiotherapist. Michael was the oldest of five, with three brothers and a sister, and their family home was always packed with hordes of people. Sunday lunch was always a major event. His mother tried, but usually failed, to keep the numbers under thirty. I have no idea how she coped, but I loved being there and being part of it. Everyone would be welcomed – cousins would arrive from New Zealand and stay for years, and the house was always full. Yet despite the presence of so many people, no one fought. They were an incredibly happy and entertaining family.

My own family was a little more complex. My parents had married when they were both twenty-one. They were an exquisite couple: she was stunningly beautiful, while he was dashing and very aristocratic, coming from a family sprinkled with titles and royal connections. My sister Caroline, known as Cara, was born within a year and I followed eighteen months later. For the first few years of our lives we lived in luxury. We had a Georgian house in Chelsea, a country cottage in Wiltshire, two cars and lots of holidays – skiing in winter, the Mediterranean in the summer. My mother had one of the largest and most fashionable wardrobes in London and was a famous beauty. We children were looked after by nannies; our parents were glamorous figures who appeared from time to time and then disappeared almost instantly.

Then when I was four and Cara six the marriage broke up. My mother had developed an interest in psychology, which helped lead to her rejection of my father. Not long afterwards my father left and went to live in Germany. Apart from one brief meeting a couple of years later, we didn't see him again until I was fifteen. Overnight our lives changed dramatically, as he refused to support us. We moved to a small, rather grim flat and were sent to a succession of schools – nine by the time I was twelve. Despite my father's initial promise that he would at least pay for school fees, he reneged on his word; so every time the money ran out, we had to move on. But it took a while to realise that the money would never be forthcoming and so we were moved from one fee-paying school to another; although later, about seven schools down the line, I also attended a state school for a year. My sister managed to keep up with her studies but the constantly changing schools and curricula – one would teach German, the next French – left me floundering, and I learned very little.

My mother never mentioned our father and there were no photographs, so over time he became a mystery figure. All I had were a few hazy memories. I remember going fishing with him at our cottage in Wiltshire. He had painstakingly made beautiful feather flies and would sit for hours waiting for trout to bite and then wade into the water in his long boots. I remember him dressing up as Father Christmas one year, and I remember him cooking sausages. I didn't like them and hid them in the umbrella stand.

None of our relations helped us. My mother came from a devoutly Catholic family where the fear of mortal sin ruled. Her parents didn't take too kindly to the divorce and we were effectively ostracised, while my father's family, at least the aristocratic members of it, were too grand to mix with the offspring of a divorce.

My mother, desperate and lonely with two small children, struggled to manage. She had very little interest in cooking – the nannies had done all that sort of thing before. Neither my sister nor I was particularly keen on eating, and I remember her dyeing our food blue to tempt us to eat it. Cara and I often slept in our school uniforms. We couldn't be bothered to undress, and our mother never seemed to notice such things. Once a month she would decide it was time to tidy us up and brush our hair. This took much yanking on her part and screaming on ours, and eventually she would snip out the worst of the knots. We must have looked a bizarre sight, but no one ever commented.

Eventually she remarried – to an old childhood friend, John Francis, known as JF. He had been a monk for thirteen years and had taught at Ampleforth, the Catholic school for boys. But having decided that holy orders were not for him, he was delighted to find that our mother was available. They married very quickly, and my sister and I were bridesmaids.

We hated him. He wanted to be with our mother and didn't want two small girls around. Many battles ensued. He used to 'fine' us by forbidding us to watch our favourite television programmes. In a remarkably short space of time we had accrued so many 'fines' that we were banned from TV for life. The TV went and war began. We cut holes in his pants, hid his glasses and wiped our noses on his side of the bed. I was definitely the ringleader and spent many hours devising ways to annoy him.

JF went to work for the Russian section of the BBC and our house was constantly filled with drunken Russians dancing with wine bottles on their heads. Most of them smashed on the carpet, leaving wine stains everywhere. Cara and I watched through the bannisters, thoroughly entertained. Our younger sister, Tilly, arrived when I was thirteen. She was a strong-willed child, who looked just like her father. Meanwhile Cara had developed scoliosis, or curvature of the spine, and had to wear a rigid back brace. It was torture for her and complicated our relationship. We had been incredibly close as small children but, angry that she was suffering while I had escaped, and despite her brilliance at school and my ineptitude, towards our late teens she became increasingly distant from me.

Eventually JF and our mother separated and divorced. Then he married the mother of two of his other children, who promptly left him and went to live in New Zealand.

He had by that time turned to the law and taken his Bar exams, and he moved swiftly on to a trainee barrister a third of his age. The relationship came to a sudden end when she expressed a desire for children. He decided, perhaps understandably, that he'd got quite enough already.

When I was fifteen and Cara seventeen our father suddenly got in touch and said he wanted to meet us. He was living in Paris with his second wife, a Danish woman. They had married in Copenhagen Cathedral when she was six months pregnant, and determined to get a ring on her finger and have a white wedding. The ring turned out to be one my father had given my mother as a gift for having my sister Cara, and which she had returned to him with the rest of her jewellery when they parted, in the hope that he would behave decently. I fear my father was dragged reluctantly down the aisle, never having really got over my mother. He and my stepmother went on to have two children, but she was reluctant to include Cara and me in this second family.

So now Cara and I set off for Paris full of excitement and trepidation. We spent some time wandering round the Gare du Nord, where he was supposed to meet us, approaching strangers and asking if they were our father. Eventually he came running down the platform and we introduced ourselves. By then my father was a wealthy banker. But we were not invited into this new-found wealthy world – it became one we could watch but not participate in. After that visit we saw our father sporadically, but never with any predictability or for long.

When I met Michael I wanted to keep my background

secret. It all felt too complicated to explain and I felt ashamed. But Michael, being no fool, worked out the full picture for himself. After his own upbringing it was rather a shock. But we learned to laugh about it together, though the hurt I felt was immense and he knew it.

My mother liked him instantly. I think she was relieved that he was such a contrast to my last boyfriend, and she was genuinely happy for me. But when it came to planning the wedding she was desperately distracted with her new boyfriend, a tall, dark and handsome married man. My stepfather, meanwhile, was busy chasing the next object of his affections. And my father, having offered to foot the bill, was soon back-pedalling as fast as his legs could go. All weddings are a nightmare to organise, but ours had to take the prize for absolute chaos.

When my father announced that he wanted to be involved in my wedding, I was thrilled after so many years of not belonging. How naïve I was! My father was a sentimentalist at heart, but had a very tight pocket. The result was that he was torn between trying to 'do the right thing' for my wedding and his desire not to spend any money. It was bound to end in tears.

First of all, having taken not the blindest bit of interest in any aspect of my wellbeing to date, my father decided that he wished to scrutinise my husband-to-be. Poor Michael was packed off to the Cavalry Club for a daunting lunch-plus-interrogation. He felt as though he was going to see the headmaster for six of the best, and wondered whether he should put exercise books in the seat of his trousers as a precaution. His anxiety was justified. He returned feeling that he had been marked down as 'trade' and not deemed at all suitable – not an auspicious start to his relationship with his future father-in-law.

Then, in planning the wedding, my father became fanatical in his pursuit of minimal cost and maximum glamour. We wanted a very traditional ceremony and arranged to be married in St Mary's, Cadogan Place, followed by a reception at the Cavalry Club. I had chosen Cadogan Place in Chelsea because my parents had married there, and I really wanted to make up for the fact that their marriage had failed. As it was a Catholic church Michael, an Anglican, had to take instruction in the details of Catholicism. We went for classes with a delightful and eccentric priest, Monsignor George Tancred.

So far all was going well, apart from the fact that the budget was seriously distressing my father. We'd managed to whittle the bill down to a sum which meant that there wouldn't be too many guests and they'd probably all be drinking fizzy water, but my father desperately wanted a Master of Ceremonies. It really mattered to him. If it meant that no one ate, so be it – at least they would be announced.

Eight weeks before the wedding, with the invitations printed, Michael and I went to India on a Spink business trip. We planned to send out the invitations when we got back. On our return we were greeted by my mother at the airport, asking gaily, 'How do you fancy getting married in Kent?' My father, it seemed, had backed out of the wedding completely and disappeared. He just couldn't take the strain of parting with any money.

My mother, rising to the occasion, had contacted old family friends, the parents of one of her godchildren, and asked whether we could get married from their house. They were gracious and generous, and said it would be a practice run for when their own daughter got married. We obtained a large and decorative special licence from the Archbishop of Canterbury to enable us to marry at the village church in Appledore, Kent, but I was incredibly disappointed that we weren't married in a Catholic church. In those days it was very important to me.

My stepfather now agreed to step in and give me away. Despite our difficult relationship in the early years, we had grown fond of each other. JF was a larger-than-life character who ate and drank too much, was a great raconteur and spoke eight languages. Women were his weakness, but no matter what he did he had a sort of penitent look – it probably came with being a monk – which made you forgive him.

On our wedding day my father turned up at the last minute, looking distinctly dishevelled. JF graciously stepped aside and, after borrowing a waistcoat and some cufflinks (which he never returned), my father accompanied me in the wedding car where he wept sentimentally and told me how sorry he was for everything. I think for those ten minutes he felt genuinely saddened, though I was to see him only twice more in the eleven years before he died.

Despite all the hitches we had a beautiful May wedding. A girlfriend had made me a raw silk wedding dress embroidered with pearls, full and flowing, and I felt wonderful in it. I had four bridesmaids, including eleven-year-old Tilly, and the sun shone throughout. We had around 250 guests and the atmosphere was wonderful, despite the fact that half of them weren't speaking to the other half and my mother was only just prevented from throwing a glass of champagne over my stepmother after she froze out my mother's attempted polite conversation.

When we got to the speeches my father had disappeared, perhaps daunted by the fact that the past he had tried to bury was here in full force. But it didn't matter. JF gave a wonderful speech and so did Michael's brother Patrick. At the end of the day we left in Michael's little MG, known as the TT, or 'Tart Trap', trailing a 'Just Married' sign and hundreds of tin cans. After the bedlam of the wedding a fortnight in Bali alone with Michael seemed like untold bliss. That was, until I started throwing up and realised that our baby was on the way.

Chapter 2

Those months preparing for the arrival of our baby were among the happiest Michael and I ever had. I loved being pregnant and I stayed fit and active throughout. I didn't put on weight until the nausea stopped, but after that I seriously made up for it. I wish someone had warned me not to eat for England because I put on five stone. By the end I was actually waddling and my bump stuck out in front of me like a football.

This would be the first grandchild for both sides and everyone thought it would be a boy. Michael's mother, having produced four boys herself, made her preference absolutely clear and insisted on referring to my bump as 'him' – she wouldn't even entertain the thought that it was a girl. This made me just a little nervous that I might let the side down if the 'him' turned out to be a 'her', though for my own part I didn't actually mind what sex the baby was. My own mother was still very distracted by her love affair, but was happy for me. My sister Cara, with whom I'd had a love-hate relationship for the past few years, came round to the whole idea and was very supportive towards the end.

I worked in my studio until a couple of weeks before I was due. I much preferred to stay busy and fill my days. And they were full because I'd also been putting my stamp on the little house in Battersea. After installing a new kitchen we decorated the baby's room. Among our wedding presents we had received two sets of very expensive champagne glasses, and we swapped one set for a wonderful cot. I can still recall the feeling I had when it arrived. It was huge, painted white and had gracefully curved ends. Looking at it, standing ready, it was as though the reality of the pregnancy hit me. Soon a real person would be lying in that cot – it was over-whelming but wonderful at the same time.

I was attending antenatal classes at the West London and Hammersmith Hospital. It was extremely dilapi-dated and due for closure, but I liked it. Despite the scruffiness it was friendly, warm and welcoming. The classes were great fun. They genuinely appeased my terror at the prospect of giving birth and at the same time introduced me to a bunch of really nice girls. We spent most of the time laughing.

Towards the end of the classes partners were invited to join a session. The fathers-to-be duly turned up, most of them looking highly embarrassed and hiding their red faces behind nervous laughs. Michael bantered with the rest but said afterwards that he had learned a lot too. I realise now that the prospect of imminent parenthood must have been just as terrifying for him as it was for me, though at the time I was too absorbed in my own feelings to give this much thought.

My due date came and went. Fed up and tired of waiting, I was uncomfortable and getting more and more nervous. I'd much rather have done without all the earth-mother processes and gone and bought a baby at Tesco.

When there was no sign of anything happening by 26 January, the tenth day after my baby was due, I went into hospital to be induced. Much to my surprise, I was told that I was already in labour. The contractions I'd been having were mild, and I'd assumed they were the normal Braxton Hicks practice contractions that happen during the last months of pregnancy.

A lovely midwife broke my waters and told me, 'That'll speed things up.' It sure did – I went off to have a hot bath and within minutes I had gone from the odd mild contraction to one every minute. It was agony – I couldn't believe this was happening to me. I removed myself as quickly as I could from the bath, praying that things would slow down again – this was far too painful. Back in my little room I gasped gas and air and didn't let go of Michael's hand. I squeezed it so hard I'm surprised I didn't snap a few bones. Having said that, I still think men get off mighty lightly when it comes to childbirth and should be made, at the very least, to have their legs waxed while their partners are suffering.

Painful though the whole business was, I got through it without uttering a peep. I'd heard plenty of stories of banshee-like women screaming their guts out and felt this to be totally undignified. I decided I'd rather suffer quietly, and I did – so much so that the midwife said she'd never had a more silent patient. Anticipating that my labour would last the average fifteen hours, I had packed endless sandwiches for Michael to plough his way through during the expected marathon. As it was, he had some serious eating to do since my labour was short and straightforward – four hours from beginning to end.

Henry was born to the sound of Mozart. He popped out, gave a great roar and promptly peed on Michael. A fine start to the parental relationship! He was handed straight to me. After the effort of pushing him into the world I looked down at this slippery little creature in my arms. There are no words to describe that first moment. I can't think of any instance in my life that has equalled the first time I looked into Henry's eyes. It was a meeting of souls which touched every nerve and fibre of my being. I felt I recognised him – it was as if he stirred a memory within me. I remember feeling incredulous – this was our son, we had created him together, and the enormity of it was hard to take in. I loved this little person instantly and felt so very proud. Michael was grinning from ear to ear.

We hadn't yet decided what to call him. Despite sifting through books of babies' names, nothing had really appealed. A friend in the art world who was fanatical about all things Victorian had offered to pay his school fees if we called him Augustus. Luckily for him, we didn't! Once our son was born we both felt he just looked like a Henry and it was immediately settled. It was nothing to do with my name – in fact we didn't even think of the connection.

Henry scored high on the Apgar chart, a measurement that rates the child's first responses. But simultaneously the doctors were rushing round me – the third stage of labour was not happening. They needed to operate immediately to remove the placenta. Consent forms were rushed in. I was shaking with exhaustion and shock and could hardly understand what was going on. It was all happening very fast. I didn't want to be parted from

Henry, but as I disappeared into the operating theatre they handed him to a nurse and assured me they'd clean him up and dress him.

The procedure was quick, and I was soon reunited with my baby on the ward and encouraged to breastfeed him. I tried, but with no success at all – he wouldn't latch on. The nurses said he was just a lazy baby and that I should try tickling his feet to wake him up while feeding. I tried this and everything else I could think of, but nothing worked. I began to feel like a failure, since all the other mothers on the ward seemed to be managing fine. But I was just told to relax and try again in the morning.

By the second day I was worried because not only was Henry still not feeding, he hadn't woken at all. The paediatricians did the usual checks and said that all was fine and he was just lazy. They seemed quite relaxed about this, assuring me that it was a common occurrence and that he'd wake up and begin to feed soon. But when he hadn't breastfed by the third day I was handed a bottle of formula milk to feed him. Bottles are far easier for babies to take since much less sucking is involved. Henry gulped it down, compounding my feelings of failure.

I felt lonely and afraid. Something was nagging at the back of my mind; some distant memory was beckoning. I felt a sense of dread. When I was about nine years old I'd watched an old black and white film about Helen Keller, a girl who was deaf, dumb and blind. With the help of her wonderful teacher, who wouldn't give up on her, Helen had finally managed to break through the fog of her disability. She went on to learn several foreign languages and live a full and remarkable life. While watching this film a funny thing had happened. I suddenly knew I would do the same thing, and bring a child out of darkness. I didn't have any inkling that it would be my own child, only that somehow it would happen. The memory of this vision faded over the years but came back to haunt me now as I stared down at my beautiful, sleeping, newborn son. Could this be the nagging memory? Could this be the child?

After six days – a normal stay for a new mum in those days – Henry and I left hospital. He was still asleep but had somehow passed his pre-going home hospital check, and I had been assured that all was well. He looked gorgeous and was a good weight, so perhaps this was what convinced the medical staff that he was fine.

It was wonderful to take him home to our little house and put him into the beautiful cot waiting in his room. But our nagging doubts continued over the days and weeks to follow. Henry rarely opened his eyes, and if he did it was momentary and they weren't focussed at all.

Feeding him was a nightmare. I resorted to expressing milk, which I found excruciating, and then bottling it and feeding him. He never cried for a feed, so I set the clock every four hours. He didn't wake while feeding but gently and oh so slowly sucked the bottle. It often took two and a half hours to feed him. In complete frustration at his slowness I virtually cut off the tip of the teat so that he would be obliged to swallow more quickly. He choked at first, but he did begin to swallow a little better.

This endless feeding cycle was very time-consuming and depressing. But what really upset me was that I was getting no reaction from him at all. There was no eye contact, no hint of a first smile. His eyes remained firmly shut and the loneliness of holding and feeding a baby who never looked at me was unbearable.

By six weeks I felt there was a problem with Henry and voiced my concerns to friends. Mostly they avoided saying anything, and in any case few of them were parents so they knew very little about what babies should or shouldn't be doing. The grandparents also said very little – perhaps they didn't want to see that there was a problem, or wanted to protect our feelings. Henry looked bonny, was growing well and had no odd or unusual features; he simply wasn't functioning as a baby ought. So they wisely or cleverly kept quiet.

At three months I took him back to the hospital for his twelve-week check. He passed, though I cannot imagine how. He was bonny and had grown, but he was also floppy and inert and still hadn't really woken. A few days later I had a reunion with my antenatal group. All the babies were much the same age – but what a difference between their babies and mine. At three months these babies were enchanting and engaging. They smiled, gurgled, wriggled and looked around them with interest, reacting to every face that came close.

I literally ran from this meeting, my heart pounding. Now I was certain that Henry had a problem. I went to our local medical practice and was seen immediately by one of the GPs. She looked at Henry, prodded him and then got a little box out and waved a raisin in front of Henry's unfocused eyes. He didn't follow it, and after about a minute of waving it around in front of my son she bluntly announced that she believed he had brain damage. At that moment I shrank. My whole being screamed in agony – I couldn't take in what she was saying. Brain damage to me meant 'vegetable'. I wanted to cry, but forced myself to remain outwardly calm. I asked for a referral to a specialist and she said it would probably mean a two-month wait.

I raced home, clutching Henry tightly to me, my mind numb with shock and disbelief. I rang Michael at the office, told him that our son probably had brain damage, and asked him to come home. I wept with fear – what would happen to us and our beloved son? I couldn't face the agony of waiting to know. When Michael got home we headed straight for St George's, our local hospital. Forget the referral – after receiving such devastating news we weren't going to wait for some polite letter giving us an appointment somewhere in the distant future. All our preconceived ideas flew out of the window. Everyone fantasises for their children, but now all we could see was a big black void filled with waves of fear and terror at such an unquantifiable future.

At the hospital we were lucky enough to be seen by the senior paediatric consultant. We must have been looking terribly miserable and amazingly they accommodated us immediately. He manipulated Henry, looked into his eyes and checked his reflexes, and said yes, there was a problem, but that it wasn't obvious what it was. He told us that we should take him home, allow him to develop and bring him back when he was about a year old. They would then be able to assess more accurately how he had done with all the first-stage milestones.

Waiting has never been my strong point, but I had no choice. Internally I wept with fear and frustration. I couldn't believe that I could have no answers – surely someone would have some ideas as to what could be wrong? I couldn't understand why they hadn't offered Henry any tests. My mind was filled with a trillion questions, and I was left with no one to ask and no one to reassure me or tell me everything would be all right. We were on our own.

The months passed by in a blur. I felt incredibly lonely. I had this beautiful but inert baby and I spent hours wandering round parks, pushing his pram and not really knowing what to do. I tried to appear happy and put on a brave face, but inside felt sick to the core. I didn't really talk to anyone. I was so filled with terror that I wanted to bury my head in the sand. I didn't want to admit to anyone, not even my own family, that there was a problem. It was as though I thought it would go away if I never spoke of it. And although Michael and I did talk about it sometimes there wasn't much we could say – apart from speculating about what might be wrong, which scared the hell out of both of us.

Every time I looked down at Henry I couldn't believe that he was damaged in any way. This was my baby, my perfect baby. I'd had such high hopes for him – it just couldn't be true. The trouble was I had the evidence – it only took one glance at another baby to see the truth, but I couldn't reconcile myself to it. Those first few months were an internal nightmare of conflicting emotions. One minute I denied there was anything wrong and was sure that he'd pick up. The next I drowned in a sea of terror at the unknown prospect of dealing with a disabled child with no clear future ahead.

Then, when Henry was six months old, I bumped into a friend who suggested we visited a doctor with 'special sight'. I was a little puzzled by this and not at all sure, but I decided we had nothing to lose, so I rang the number and booked an appointment. I told Michael I wanted him to come too – I wasn't going on my own. We were surprised to discover that the address was near Piccadilly Circus, in an office above the Café Royal. A strange place for a doctor to be working. We duly arrived at the appointed hour to find 'Psychic' printed in large letters on the door. We thought there must be some mistake – where was the doctor? We debated whether to do a quick U-turn, and then caught one another's eye and laughed. We'd never given the idea of psychics or mediums much thought and both had an inherent cynicism towards the subject, but having come this far we decided to give it a go. And I had to admit to being just a little bit curious.

The woman we met had long frizzy hair and looked suitably witch-like. Henry was asleep in his buggy looking completely healthy and without a care in the world. The scene was set. We all sat down and she switched on a tape.

With hindsight this meeting was truly extraordinary, though at the time I found the information she gave us hard to deal with. She knew nothing at all about us, yet got a huge amount right. She started off by chatting about our house being near the river, but at this point I wasn't convinced because half the houses in London are near the river. She went on to Michael and said, accurately, that he was in the art world and dealing with artefacts from the Far East. She talked of a partner and setting up a business.

After a while she moved on to me. She spoke of me being involved with politics and writing a book. Then she talked about Henry. She started off by saying, ''E looks all right, don't 'e?' Then she said, 'Minerals and vitamins could starve the brain.' After some ums and ers she went on, 'Don't be worried by 'is semi-spastic state – 'e'll grow out of it and 'e'll take further education.' She went on saying that he would 'grow out of it', but she didn't say how.

I was horrified. 'Semi-spastic?' He wasn't showing any signs of something so awful. When we got home I threw the tape in a drawer – I wanted to forget what she'd said.

Soon after this Michael and I decided to try for another baby. He and his brothers and sister were all very close, and we both wanted a handful of children. And although we were naturally a little worried, we'd been told that there was no reason to think that another child would have any problems.

After a couple of months we found to our joy that I was pregnant again. But our elation was short-lived. When we went for my first scan at twelve weeks the radiographer looked at the screen in a very concentrated fashion. She didn't look comfortable, didn't say much and went off to find someone. Michael shifted uneasily beside me; we both knew this didn't bode well. Soon a consultant arrived, and after looking at the scan told us that he could find no heartbeat. Our baby was dead.

It's funny how one minute you can be filled with joy

and the next you're ripped apart. The next day I was in the operating theatre for a termination. Feeling angry and a failure, I went home to my sleeping baby.

When you're in the midst of loss and grief it's easy to become isolated, and I felt that our 'bad luck' was starting to do that to Michael and me. We found it hard to relate to other people's happy families when ours seemed to be going so disastrously wrong. We went through incredible patches of loneliness. We cut ourselves off from friends and family. We went through so many emotions, from tremendous guilt to great fear to grief and humiliation. We felt mystified about why this should happen to us, and we couldn't help feeling that we'd done something to cause one child to be damaged and another to die *in utero*.

How could we possibly be socially acceptable with this turmoil going on in us? Unconsciously perhaps, we knew that our lives were diverging from the norm. It was beginning to feel as if we were living on a different planet. We didn't feel that any of our friends could identify with what we were going through; why should they? We had less and less in common with them. We'd meet up with friends and there would be an awkwardness – they wouldn't know what to say to us, though I'm sure they felt sympathy. The trouble was, we didn't want sympathy; we just wanted to be ordinary, to be like everyone else. In time this sense of isolation began to pass and we did learn to touch base with other people and to laugh again, but in those early days we felt terribly alone.

Henry was coming up to his first birthday. We had a wonderful birthday party at Granny's in Surrey and the whole family came. By then Henry's cousins Vicky and Adam had been born, so there were three grandchildren, and although everyone could see that Henry was not like the other children it wasn't discussed.

By now it was clear that something was very wrong. Henry hadn't passed any milestones at all. He had no head control, plainly couldn't see, and couldn't sit un-aided or do anything for himself. He still looked abso-lutely gorgeous, however, and he did have one sense very fully developed – he had hyper-acute hearing. He jumped at the slightest sound and loud noises would leave him wailing in agony. We had to be very careful to keep things quiet around him. We began playing him soft classical music and discovered that he loved it. He would listen, entranced, for hours and even at this early age he could tap out a rhythm, however obscure.

Now that Henry was one we were able to take him back to the hospital, where they suggested various tests to try to identify his condition. They tested him for chromosomal abnormalities – there were none. Then they booked him in for a CAT scan which would X-ray his brain and show up any damage. The doctors assumed he had brain damage in both the motor and visual parts of his brain, and so, I guess, did we.

We had to wait several months for the CAT scan, and meanwhile I found I was pregnant again. We were happy, but anxious too. Surely this time everything would be fine – it just had to be. I needed something to hold on to, to give us hope. It's hard looking after a baby who doesn't respond at all. I longed to be a real mother.

Once I was twelve weeks pregnant we traipsed off to the hospital again for my scan. The radiographer smiled at us and remembered us from the last time. But as soon as I was on the table and the scan began her smile disappeared and it all felt horribly *déjà vu*. Just like the time before, she disappeared from the room without saying a word.

Michael and I looked at one another. You could have cut the unspoken dread with a knife. We waited in silence for the consultant, who studied the scan. Then he turned to us and explained that the baby had a tumour covering the entirety of its spine and would probably not survive the pregnancy. If it did survive to full term it would almost certainly not survive in the operating theatre afterwards. He suggested that the best option was a termination. He explained that this condition frequently went with a chromosomal abnormality and, considering our track record, it would be worth getting a genetic reading done. This would involved inserting a needle through the cervix and taking a sample of the fluid surrounding the baby.

I felt numb with grief. I wanted this baby even if it did have problems, but knowing it might well die seemed too awful a risk to take. I felt utterly torn. I wasn't sure I could stay sane and survive a whole pregnancy with a virtual guarantee of death at birth.

Michael and I discussed it all at great length. He was completely supportive and always believed that I should make the final decision. He would have supported me either way, and said so. I was free to choose. I walked beside the river for a couple of days, agonising over what to do. And finally I decided to terminate the pregnancy.

Eight weeks later Henry had his CAT scan. The same look of concentration crossed the radiographers' faces – I'd seen it twice before. Human nature has a funny habit of echoing itself. They peered at Henry's scans more closely and they peered at Henry. These scans did not match the severely disabled child lying on the bed. No damage showed. Henry's brain appeared to be perfect.

Chapter 3

When we arrived home we sat in stunned silence. Neither of us could think of a single thing to say. The past six months had weighed heavily. The two lost pregnancies and the prospect that Henry was brain-damaged had drawn us into our own private world of misery. Now suddenly, like a fresh breeze blowing in on a warm spring evening, there it was, a whisper of hope again.

Hope is one of the most painful emotions – it knows no boundaries. When you hope you engage in a roller-coaster ride of emotions. One minute you soar, the next you plummet. I know that for many people it's easier to give up, accept the way things are and get on with life as best you can. But when the CAT scan offered us hope for Henry, something deep inside me began to awaken. It was as though I was recalling who I was and why I was here. I saw uncertainty as a gift and an adventure. I knew that, by keeping my mind open, anything or anybody could be introduced into the equation. I was prepared to knock on doors and to explore every possibility of a cure for my son. I knew I had a mission.

When I had given birth to Henry I had had a vision of him as a young man standing in a library. The shelves were oak, and I could see Henry holding a book open and silently reading from it. A ray of light shone across his head – I could pick out dust particles in the air. I could see what he was wearing – cords and a jumper – and it felt like spring. This vision has never faded.

After the visit to the medium when Henry was six months old I'd been horrified at the thought of a 'semi-spastic child' and had rejected everything she had said. At the time Henry was a small baby and his disability hadn't yet manifested clearly. But now it had, and he was classified as severely disabled. I dug the medium's tape out of the drawer and listened to it again. In the light of all that had happened, her words seemed extraordinary. It was if she was reminding me of who I was, of my capabilities and my journey. Unbeknown to her, she gave me the courage to believe in the vision that I'd had at Henry's birth. I found it hard to understand why my vision should be confirmed by a medium sitting in a shabby rented office above the Café Royal. But this was just the first of many profound 'coincidences' which life has introduced at every step of our journey.

Looking after Henry was neither hard nor easy – it remained lonely. I hadn't worked since his birth, but when he was a few months old I began to long to go back to bookbinding. I needed people – I needed stimulation and I needed to be creative again. My elder sister Cara was by then head of frescoes at English Heritage and she knew many picture restorers. She introduced me to a wonderful studio in Holland Park where I began work, sharing the space with three picture restorers. At first I brought Henry with me. He lay asleep all day in his moses basket, which I carefully placed on top of the guillotine we used for cutting card.

The three picture restorers, Sarah, Jenny and Zahira, were lovely girls. We gossiped for most of the day and only stopped chatting for very important radio programmes such as *The Archers* and *Woman's Hour*, or for our frequent visits to the ice-cream shop next door. I felt happy and vaguely in control. I remained self-employed but worked pretty well exclusively for David Khalili, the Iranian dealer I had worked for before Henry's birth. Every few weeks I'd go and collect a pile of the most stunning manuscripts, take them back to the studio and restore them. Slowly my spirit returned.

So far I had kept my vision for Henry to myself, but now I began to voice it. To me it was as clear as crystal, and telling people about it made it more real. Some people pitied me – I could see the look in their eyes. Others championed me. It was really a 50/50 divide between those who found it painful to hope and discouraged my dreams for Henry, and those who were open-minded and gamely supported me.

My mother found it incredibly hard to believe in my vision for Henry. She wanted to, but couldn't bring herself to in case the worst happened, and she saw me being torn apart by the pain of failure. My faith and hers were on the line; mine amounted to believing in a miracle, and hers dared not. Cara was gently supportive – her heart told her I was probably talking rubbish but she knew me better than that and trusted my sincerity. She'd always say, 'If that's what you believe, then that's what counts.' Michael's mother was much more open and very spiritual. Whether she believed in my vision or not I couldn't really say, but she was prepared to listen and talk to me about it – she wasn't at all antagonistic, and I felt she believed me. She also sent me books which supported my beliefs.

I couldn't go on taking Henry to work for ever, so we employed a lovely seventeen-year-old nanny, Debbie – a girl from India who had the largest pair of bosoms I'd ever seen. She had glossy black hair, a huge smile and a strong penchant for sweeties. She literally enveloped Henry and adored him from day one. This freed me up to work half days – some semblance of normality was returning to my life.

At this stage Henry woke a few times a day for tiny bursts of time and was eating some solid food, though he preferred puree. He had also begun having fits. About once a month, when he was deeply relaxed, he would have a giggle fit in which he'd tighten up and giggle for a few minutes. At this stage we didn't worry much about it, but by the age of two he was having other types of fits and they became far more frequent, until he was having up to thirty a day. They were always brief, and often just consisted of a few moments in which Henry would appear 'absent'. We were referred through St George's to the neurology department of another hospital where he was wired up to an electroencephalograph (EEG). He actually had several fits while wired up, but they didn't register at all. The woman doing the EEG had to check that her machine was working properly. She had never seen someone have such obvious fits which didn't register. This meant that Henry wasn't epileptic, but simply had unidentified fits.

Our paediatrician, Professor David Hall, remained

mystified by our son and carried Henry's notes with him at all times, just in case he came up with anything that might give a clue to his problems. David knew that both of us hated check-ups at the hospital and sensitively and generously accommodated our feelings by visiting us at home. To this day I appreciate this kindness.

Henry was offered physiotherapy on the National Health Service and began to receive weekly treatment from a very special physiotherapist called Chris Bungay. Her gentleness surpassed all expectation, and her quiet acceptance of our dreams for Henry ensured that no meeting with us was ever clouded. This was my first experience of a true healer at work; it was as if we could just 'be' in her presence – there was no judgement. Watching her work with Henry permeated all of us with a sense of wellbeing and tremendous peace. We knew we were lucky to have her, and she still remains a close friend.

In my quest for solutions I started to read. I worked my way through biology books, biochemistry books, anything I could lay my hands on. I remember at school getting just above zero in a biology exam. I couldn't really see the point of leaf osmosis. Who on earth cares? I certainly didn't. But now, faced with the prospect of being the sole 'searcher' for Henry, I was prepared to get stuck into any amount of reading, however boring. If it could shed just one tiny glimmer of light, or show me which direction I could go in, it would be worth it. I felt my education was only just beginning.

Michael knew how strongly I felt and was happy to let me get on with this research. He would follow what I was doing and discuss it with me but didn't initiate any of the searching, perhaps because he felt bemused by all that had happened and uncertain about the direction we should follow. He knew my instinct was strong and he supported me, but I'm sure he had doubts. After all, finding a cure for Henry was my internal vision – how could he possibly trust that I was really going to be right? It was I who believed in miracles and, although Michael wanted to believe with me, he felt torn.

Michael was now working very long hours and I was tired of the isolation I felt with Henry. I wanted to mix with other parents of disabled children but had no real way of meeting them. I didn't really want to mix with regular kids – my emotion were too raw, and I couldn't face sitting there like a miserable blob while other people's kids ran around and mine didn't. I knew the choice in that situation would be to sit there, say nothing and take it on the chin or start saying I had a vision for Henry and sound like a wishful-thinking mother. I felt I couldn't win, and I didn't want to see the looks of pity on their faces.

I had one particular friend who had produced a healthy son at the same time as Henry was born. I couldn't believe how she gloated over her son's abilities whenever we met. She boasted without drawing breath, while my child lay inert on the ground. I'm quite capable of celebrating success with the next person, but this was simply rubbing my nose in it. The pain she caused me was immense, yet I don't think she had a clue. I stopped seeing her after a while – I dare say she labelled me paranoid! But I simply couldn't deal with other people's insensitive behaviour or their emotions. It was hard enough to deal with my own.

Hiding our misery and appearing cheerful and upbeat in public was proving to be an uphill struggle for both Michael and me. We fought a lot. I still very much wanted the normal pleasures in life such as going on holiday or out to the theatre – I wanted to be distracted; whereas Michael wanted to cope by burying himself in work. We had no way of dealing with or channelling our immense feelings of loss, and the result was that we directed a lot of anger at each other. I remember feeling very justified in my anger at the time, and utterly confident that I was being totally reasonable and that Michael was being a complete ostrich and very obstinate to boot. No doubt he felt the same about me!

Chris, our physiotherapist, could see and feel the tension between us. She discreetly suggested that we visit a counsellor at St George's Hospital. I felt a great sense of sadness that we had to resort to this, but at the same time relief that someone might be able to help us. Michael didn't really want to know, but reluctantly agreed to go along. I'm afraid some pride came into it – neither of us liked admitting that we were flummoxed by what had been thrown at us.

There was no one available to counsel adults in our situation, so we were referred to the children's psychiatric department. We felt rather uncomfortable about this. None the less we turned up and were ushered into a very shabby, box-like room. A young man poked his head around the door, came in and sat down rather nervously – he didn't look much older than me! He turned out to be a very gentle and inviting young therapist, whom I immediately warmed to. This was the first time I had felt free to express how I really felt and to start trying to unravel the complexities of my emotions. I found it relatively easy to open up and begin to talk, but Michael found it very hard. I'm afraid this gave me the upper hand in manipulating the situation to my advantage. I looked willing and he looked obstinate.

Our marriage had hit an all-time low at this point. All I wanted was a bloody holiday, but Michael didn't. I remember we talked and talked to this poor young man – I felt he had probably never seen the like, as he was far more used to dealing with troubled kids who were probably a lot more straightforward than us. We spent several sessions having these therapeutic chats and in truth, though we were rather cynical about it at the time, I really believe it did help. We began to recognise that we couldn't just bury our heads in separate buckets of sand. Grieving takes all sorts of forms, and the most common is to shut down all forms of communication.

Michael and I both knew that we wanted to be married and we wanted to be happily married – we didn't want to drift apart. We could see that if we let things go too far we would end up total strangers with little in common, and we were both determined not to let that happen. Pain is a great divider. We had to learn to talk and to condense our quality time together. All kids dilute parental quality time, but regular kids also give huge amounts of joy as they pass milestones and grow up. Life is about inter-action, and when there is none and the picture hardly changes it's incredibly tough. It doesn't get easier as time goes by – it gets harder, because the reality of your child's lack of progress hits you afresh as he drops further and further behind other children. Over 80 per cent of parents with special needs kids separate, and I'm not surprised. The continuous stress, if it is allowed to dominate, can so easily part any couple.

We resolved not to let this happen to us. This didn't mean we didn't fight – we did. But we also learned to have respect for each other's needs and to understand that we both needed our own kinds of compensation to counteract the tremendous sadness and loss within us. I needed holidays once in a while and Michael needed to work. So we agreed to meet halfway. It wasn't all bleak – we laughed a lot and had moments of real togetherness, but in those early years it wasn't easy adapting together to such an unknown future.

Despite the grief, the anxieties and the fears, it never occurred to either of us to put Henry into care. We knew that friends and family members sometimes wondered why we hadn't chosen this option. We didn't resent them for it; we just knew it wasn't right for us – Henry was our son, we were going to care for him and that was that.

We had friends whose child was disabled as a result of a hospital error, and after much agonising they decided to put him up for adoption. We felt that this was an incredibly brave decision and fully supported them. We knew that many people would feel they were uncaring and had abandoned their child, but until you are the parent of a disabled child you can't know the anguish involved. Taking care of a disabled child can wreck lives and relationships, so sometimes giving the child up is the wiser option. Every family's decision is their own and can't be judged by others. For our friends it was the right decision; they still see their child, he is happy and they are happy. In a funny way, seeing our friends make their decision made it easier for us to see that keeping Henry was the option we wanted.

Through St George's I began to meet other parents of disabled children. I remember one mum called Alex who had the most handsome little boy called Hamish. He was about two and a half, a year older than Henry, and had cerebral palsy. Alex and I immediately hit it off, and she told me of all the weird and wacky alternative things they were up to in search of help for Hamish. I felt rather in awe – I had only seen one medium and done nothing alternative at all; in fact I hardly understood the concept. In the past I'd had no need to venture further than the conventional, but now that my back was against the wall I was prepared to look at virtually anything. It's amazing how, when the chips are truly down, one becomes so much less judgemental.

Alex opened my eyes to the trend for trying out alternative practitioners and therapies and I embraced it, with all the possibilities that this avenue opened up for Henry. In previous generations patients had regarded their doctors as gods – and some doctors regarded themselves as gods too! But this myth had by now been largely dispelled, and parents of disabled children had realised that the lack of answers from the medical establishment didn't mean they couldn't look elsewhere for help in the effort to realise their children's best potential. If they didn't do it, who else was going to?

Alex told me she'd met a wonderful healer in north London, and I decided to take Henry to her. Lilly was a

delightful lady of about ninety. She was four-foot nothing and had such a strong presence that she was like a
magnet – everyone vied to get her attention. I gathered
that a few years back she had been working selflessly out
of a one-bedroom flat, giving hands-on healing to anyone who turned up. Since then she'd been discovered by
some pop band who had decided on a whim to set her up
in sunny suburbia, where her house became packed with
all sorts of weird and wonderful healers who offered their
services for free.

The best bit was the waiting room. That's where
everyone would get together and catch up on the weekly
news. All sorts of people came – disability has no pre-
judice but strikes at random. All classes and types were
there, and all with a common cause – healing their
children. It was a great atmosphere. The power of friendship among all those lonely and bewildered parents was
like a breath of fresh air and a spark of hope. I remember
a desperate father whose dying son had an inoperable
brain tumour – the mum had left because she couldn't
cope. Then there was the cheeky little girl in a blue frock
with a massive strawberry birth mark on her face, and
the brain-damaged boy who couldn't walk. Everyone
who came found some form of release just in being there.

I felt I was leading a schizophrenic existence. The
world of the alternative embraced and encouraged us
and filled us with hope. Yet at the same time I had to mix
with normal society, which I seemed to fit into less and
less. I felt desperately muddled. I'd got a severely disabled
child and had lost two more, one that had died *in utero*
and one that had had to be terminated due to an

inoperable tumour. Why, oh why, was this happening to me? One minute I felt uplifted and on a mission, and the next bereft – and the two just didn't tally. I needed them to meet somewhere in the middle. But how?

Internally I raged at God. I felt totally abandoned. I wanted answers, and I didn't care whether they came in a spiritual or medical form. I felt there must be a reason. No religious teaching had prepared me for this. I didn't know where to begin to find answers that would satisfy my desperate and aching heart. I looked around me – everyone seemed to have normal kids. All my sisters-in-law had produced normal offspring by this time – why couldn't I? What the hell was going on? I felt persecuted. No one had any answers. I felt miserable in the world of the normal – it was too far from the waiting room in north London where I fitted in.

Away from Lilly's healing house where our dreams were encouraged, we came back down with a bump to the conventional side of things. St George's Hospital recommended that we see a geneticist. Michael and I both gulped, as neither of us wanted to know we were the cause of our child's disability. I had spent long enough feeling guilty and afraid that I had done something wrong. I know now that all new parents of disabled children feel this way, but at the time I could only torture myself, going over and over what I might have inadvertently done wrong.

We were asked to gather all sorts of information about our family histories. Michael's mum wasn't too helpful when we asked her. As far as she was concerned, their side had never had a problem, so it must be mine. I seethed with silent anger at this. Between my guilt and her accusatory hints I was thoroughly miserable. But we did eventually gather reams of family information for the geneticists. On my side we found photos and paraphernalia going back two hundred years or so. It seemed a logistical nightmare at the time, but we somehow managed to do it.

At the time of the dreaded appointment we turned up with Henry fast asleep in his buggy. We went through all the family and individual histories we could, after which three or four white-coated geneticists muttered amongst themselves for some time. On examining Henry they discovered that his hair grew in a double crown. This turned out to be their sole interest in him, and, as you can imagine, not of great medical significance to us or Henry or any future pregnancy. We sat there feeling rather perplexed. I felt my hairdresser would have had more interesting comments to make on the subject than they did.

The geneticists then suggested they ran some blood tests – none of which they expected to show anything significant. Henry didn't present any specific features which they could immediately attach to a syndrome; in fact they pointed out that he had no irregular features at all. But for lack of anything else to do they thought they might as well do the tests.

We felt we were being shunted sideways. We couldn't believe that all our documentation, so painstakingly gathered, had yielded absolutely no hint of an explanation for Henry or the other pregnancies. I felt the experts involved weren't interested and didn't care – this was just an academic exercise and we didn't really count as human beings with feelings. I found it hard to believe that they could have trained as doctors – a profession that supposedly serves humanity and thrives on compassion. Ironically, it was as if this bunch of so-called humanitarians were genetically devoid of this emotion. In the end they sent us away saying they thought there was no genetic issue or link and that our experience was probably 'bad luck'. And that was that.

This was not what we were expecting at all. On one hand it left us feeling relieved that we were, so far, not to blame. Or perhaps I should say it left me feeling relieved. Michael, like his mother, was absolutely convinced that it had nothing to do with him. This was a continual source of irritation to me – mainly because I felt quite irrationally convinced that it had to be me, and his attitude only reinforced my guilt. The turmoil within threatened to swamp me. Fortunately my work was a valuable distraction. We attended exciting and glamorous parties in the art world through Michael's work. No one knew that Henry had problems or that we had lost two other pregnancies. I didn't deliberately hide it – I just couldn't discuss it. I didn't want other people's pity. And for a little while, every now and then, it helped to be away from our heartache and out in the world, acting as though nothing was wrong.

As expected, the results of the blood tests were normal. We went back to St George's and David Hall, our paediatrician, suggested that Henry should have a more sophisticated scan, an MRI or magnetic resonance imaging scan, to see if there could be any biochemical cause or degenerative disorder to explain his problems.

Our son's two key symptoms were floppiness and sleepiness. David Hall suggested that Henry might have a myelin disorder or something called a Dopa Responsive Dystonia disorder. Dopa is one of four key neurotransmitters and affects brain processes that control movement, emotional response and ability to experience pain. I had watched the film *Awakenings*, starring Robert De Niro and Robin Williams, in which people with the latter disorder fell asleep for thirty years and, when given the correct dosage of Dopa, woke up. But Henry didn't seem, in my view, to have the same strange symptoms that these folk had. One key feature was that if you chucked a ball at these comatose victims they miraculously caught it in mid-flight, even though they were still asleep. Chuck a ball at Henry and it hit him!

The myelin disorder seemed a far more likely probability. The myelin sheath surrounds the nerves and when this deteriorates it results in multiple sclerosis or, if a child is born without it, a total lack of muscle control resulting in floppiness. One gorgeous little girl up at Lilly's had a total myelin disorder. Henry and this little girl were so similar that we thought it had to be the same problem. We agreed to be referred to Great Ormond Street Hospital for Sick Children for the MRI.

After the last miscarriage I had become increasingly desperate to have another baby. Each unfulfilled pregnancy had left a huge void within me. I longed to have a little girl with no complications. We agreed we'd try again, and after a couple of months I became pregnant. I was over the moon. I felt sure the geneticists were right – there was no genetic link and it had just been extraordinary bad luck. I was totally convinced the new baby was a healthy girl.

My GP referred me to a special unit at St Mary's, Paddington. Normally ultrasound scans are first given at twelve-plus weeks. But this was a unit for parents who had previously suffered abnormalities or miscarriages, and they began scanning much earlier. The unit was in a dingy prefab office in the basement. The walls had pictures of smiling babies grinning down at us. Those were the happy stories, but none of us parents sitting beneath them felt convinced. We just prayed our babies' photos would one day adorn those grim walls.

My first scan was done when I was just four weeks pregnant, and I felt enormous relief when I saw that there on the screen was a tiny blip, my baby, with its little heart pulsing away. I came back for another scan every week until twelve weeks, when I was transferred to St George's where they would continue my care. There I was placed under a rather arrogant consultant whom I instantly disliked. I was badgered to have an amniocentesis – an invasive test for Down's syndrome. I was only twenty-nine and not in an at-risk age bracket, nor had the geneticists given us any indication that we had a genetic problem such as Down's. The scans were showing no abnormalities and I didn't want to run the risk of losing the baby, a real possibility with an amniocentesis. When I refused to have it the consultant said, 'Well, it's not me that has to live with a Down's child.'

When the time came for my twenty-week scan I was

still banging on about having a little girl – I was totally convinced. I was even making wonderful embroidery patchwork, all in pink. By this time I'd had so many scans that we'd got to know the radiographer really well, and the poor girl must have sat there pondering whether to say something or not. In the end she said, 'Oh, this is a perfect shot of its sex – do you want to see?'

Michael peered at the screen. 'Looks pretty female to me.'

'Er . . . well . . . those are the testicles . . .'

I sat up in surprise, totally speechless. This wasn't at all what I was expecting. Bugger, I thought, I'll have to start a new patchwork!

Despite the shock of realising that my longed-for girl was a boy, I was extremely happy to be pregnant and felt very reassured by the scans. I hardly put any weight on at all this time – I'd learned the hard way that eating for two meant looking as though I was carrying six.

A few weeks after the twenty-week scan Henry's appointment at Great Ormond Street arrived. I felt a bit nervous that they might find something degenerative but thought it fairly unlikely as Henry, who was now three, was not deteriorating at all. In fact he was still exactly the same – very floppy and very sleepy.

I found Great Ormond Street daunting, clinical and impersonal. Henry needed a general anaesethic for the MRI scan so we changed him into a white gown and sat him on a trolley to be wheeled down to the scanning room. We had put numbing cream on Henry's hands where they were going to insert a line to anaesthetise him. I came in with Henry and lifted him on to the bed near the scanner. Several white-coated medics came over to us and decided to hold him so that he wouldn't wriggle when they put the line in. They tried to get the line in, and failed. They tried again and Henry began to wail. They tried again, and again and again, using his hands, his feet and even his neck. Henry was fast becoming a pincushion – I couldn't believe what they were doing to my baby. I wanted to cry but knew it wouldn't help. I wanted to gather Henry into my arms and run. All I could do was look into Henry's eyes and keep saying, 'It'll be OK.' On the eighteenth try they found a vein.

I returned upstairs to wait with Michael in the children's ward, but waiting was awful. After that torture we wondered what else they might do. Your imagination can play havoc in an anxious situation.

Eventually Henry returned, his little hands and feet covered in puncture marks. We felt so angry, but what could we do? Thank God they let us out that afternoon – I think I would have gone mad if I'd stayed there any longer. On top of the pain they'd inflicted on Henry the noise was overwhelming for him – every child in the ward had a TV going full blast.

Two weeks later we got a letter saying that Henry's brain was normal – nothing had been detected. And that was it. Here was a little boy with a normal brain who didn't function at all – yet no one appeared to be in the slightest bit interested. We were on our own with Henry.

Chapter 4

Slowly I came to terms with having another boy, and began looking forward to meeting my new son. Looking back, it's hard to imagine why I wanted a girl so badly. Perhaps I unconsciously associated disability with males, the ratio of such problems being four boys to each girl.

The constant ultrasound scans through my pregnancy kept me reassured and I even managed to go away for a short holiday with a girlfriend, Sally. Her first child, Molly, was the same age as Henry, also disabled and also undiagnosed. But unlike Henry, Molly was totally mobile and quite a handful. Her problem was that she didn't make any eye contact at all.

A friend of my stepfather's who was immensely wealthy lent us his country retreat in Oxfordshire. With its lavish white carpets and lush silk curtains it was totally unsuitable for young children. There was even a Persian carpet adorning the hand-baked Italian ceramic floor tiles in the kitchen – no stir-fries in here, clearly. He obviously wasn't used to ketchup, let alone spontaneous eruptions of puke from grubby little mouths.

Both Sally and I were pregnant, our due dates only days apart. She was totally convinced hers was a boy and was extremely content. We basked in the sunshine and chatted for hours. In the local village we bought a cheap paddling pool and filled it up, heaping in little plastic boats, none of which would be played with. Both children splashed contentedly, gurgling away in their own little worlds. By lunchtime they were both asleep, wrapped in towels on the lawn. We pottered into the kitchen to make some lunch, leaving the children asleep just a few yards away and well within earshot.

When we went back out to the terrace with our tray piled high with goodies Henry was still fast asleep but Molly had gone. Panic set in, though we knew she couldn't have gone too far. Suddenly I heard snoring. I looked round and there, fast asleep in the paddling pool, with only her nose peeking just above the surface of the water, was Molly. Both of us stared in disbelief. Molly lived by her own rules, and this was clearly her idea of pure pleasure!

After the break I returned to London feeling good. I was thirty-two weeks pregnant and still working. I took Henry up to Lilly's every Saturday, and he continued to have physiotherapy with Chris at St George's. He was now three and a half and we wanted him to mix with other children, so we were delighted when he was given a part-time place in a local nursery school. Our nanny, Debbie, took him and remained as his support during the morning sessions.

Sometimes I used to pick Henry and Debbie up, and if not they walked home. On one occasion I was waiting with all the other mums for the children to come out of the nursery. A pregnant mum sidled up to me and said, 'Hi!' I smiled and asked her how many weeks pregnant she was. She turned out to be at the same stage as me.

Then she commented that her son was sharing a part-time slot at the nursery with 'some brain-damaged boy'. Insulted and wounded, I said he didn't have brain damage and was mine, and walked away. I don't think she even thought of Henry as belonging to someone. After all, disability happened to other people, not an ordinary-looking mum standing next to her. Two weeks later she gave birth to a premature Down's boy.

By my thirty-sixth week I still hadn't put on any weight. I was eating well but it made no difference. I wasn't worried – I'd been reassured so many times that my baby was fine. But the hospital asked me to come back for a scan the following week.

I didn't see the usual radiographer, a lovely girl who was also pregnant and who had been charming and supportive. Instead I was ushered upstairs to a ward and a scan machine was wheeled in. I lay on the bed while the radiographer looked at the scan. Then he told me that the baby was lying transversely – sideways – and that this was dangerous. If I happened to go into labour early and the baby was still lying sideways the cord would slip out first and the baby could suffocate as it was being born. Then he told me that the baby looked 'thin'. He measured his limbs and said he was the right length but far too thin – he obviously wasn't thriving. The radiographer impressed upon me that the baby was at risk if I went into labour and wasn't within minutes of the hospital, and suggested I have a caesarean straight-away as the baby wasn't thriving in any case. I was booked in for the operation two days later, on 12 November, three weeks before my due date.

Michael and I rang our families and told them the news. Debbie agreed to look after Henry all day while I was in hospital, so that Michael could be with me. I packed my bag and took one last look round our bedroom. The little moses basket sat by the bed, ready for our new son. Next time I entered this room another little person would be there with me too.

The idea of a caesarean filled me with horror. I'd been so lucky with Henry's quick and easy birth and had recovered incredibly fast, but this time I was shaking with nerves. I didn't fancy a whacking great scar, and the hospital said I wouldn't be able to drive or lift anything heavy for ten weeks. How was I going to manage Henry, who now weighed a couple of stone and had to be carried everywhere?

The night before the birth I stayed in hospital. In the corner of my room was a little plastic crib waiting to be filled. I stroked my tummy and wondered what this child would be like. I imagined him looking like Henry. Although I believed that he would be fine, I had no fantasies about what he would do in later life and hadn't thought about schools – I'd done all that before Henry was born and wouldn't risk it again. Along with queues of other expectant parents, we'd put Henry's name down for the lovely little prep school we'd visited in Kensington. Boy or girl didn't matter, but disabled did. After his birth the rejection and isolation I had felt as I had to remove his name from the list was overwhelming. I didn't want to go through that again. So I made no plans and prayed for the best. At this stage schooling seemed a very minor detail in the overall scheme of things.

The next morning, with Michael at my side, I was wheeled down to a delivery room where a team awaited us. I was told to sit on the edge of the bed and curve my spine forward as much as possible to give the surgeon room to insert a needle between my spinal vertebrae for the epidural. My heart was pounding so fast with fear that I thought everyone must be able to hear it, but much to my surprise, although I felt the needle go in, it wasn't painful at all. I lay down, and after a few minutes the junior consultant pinched my stomach. I said I thought I could still feel it – I was terrified. But as she'd pinched me with something akin to a pair of pliers she knew I hadn't felt a thing or I'd have screamed the place down! The consultant under whose care I'd been placed hadn't come to a single scan and certainly wasn't here now – but I was rather glad, if truth be told, as neither Michael nor I liked him at all. Still, it was surprising, given that I was categorised as a high-risk patient, that he hadn't wanted to see any of the scans.

A little green screen was placed just in front of my face so that I couldn't see the proceedings. Michael sat on a stool next to my head. I'm not sure who was more terrified – me of being operated on, or Michael of seeing it happen. We both cowered behind the screen, clutching hands.

The operation was quick, and within seconds my baby was out. He didn't cry, and they whisked him over to a trolley at the side of the room. I could hear the paediatrician saying, 'Come on, breathe! Come on, breathe!' The junior consultant who was stitching me up started to stitch faster and with a sense of urgency. She wanted the job done before any trouble set in – I could feel it. No one was saying anything to us, but I could hear a hiccupping sound and the doctor's voice shouting an order.

Just as the junior consultant finished sewing me up my baby was passed above me, wrapped in blue paper. For a few fleeting seconds I saw him. His eyes seemed black and I shall never forget the look of anger in them – it was as if they pierced my soul. I didn't recognise him at all – he was nothing like Henry. He was as blue as the paper he was wrapped in, his tiny chest heaving as he struggled to breathe. A strange half gasp came from him and he was gone. I began to sob, but still no one said anything.

I was wheeled into a recovery room, where we were left alone. I felt sick and I wanted to scream. Where was my baby? Was he dead? The two of us waited in silence, apart from the occasional sob from me. Michael stared blankly into space. I think we knew we were on the precipice of another tragedy and were numb at the prospect of dealing with it. Our minds were blurred with the horror of being dealt yet another blow.

The anaesthetic was beginning to wear off, and the pain I was experiencing was more than I could bear. I begged Michael to find someone to give me painkillers – I thought I'd go mad with the burning, tearing pain which threatened to overwhelm me. He disappeared and eventually returned with a surly nurse who said she didn't think I needed anything. Desperate, I begged and finally she agreed to give me some pain relief. She tried finding a vein in my arm with what looked like the biggest horse needle I'd ever seen. I can tolerate a fair amount of pain and I don't normally complain, but this reduced me to sobbing almost instantly. And where was my baby? Still no one came near us or told us anything. I don't think I have ever felt so bereft.

The painkillers didn't work and I was in agony. Two hours had now elapsed without any information. I feared the worst and felt numb with grief. Michael disappeared again in search of news, though he had no idea where to go or where our baby had been taken.

When he came back he said they'd told him they were X-raying the baby and that it didn't look good. Then he sat on the bed and wept. I don't think I'd ever seen him weep before – in fact I don't think I'd ever seen any man weep like that. It was the raw weeping of an animal. In some curious way it jolted me back into reality, and my own grief and fear were overwhelmed by anger. What on earth was going on, and why weren't we being told? It had been four hours and no one had come to talk to us.

We had argued over names before our baby was born. We had wanted to call him Max, but my mother insisted this was a dog's name and so we changed it to Freddie. Michael's grandfather then protested that Freddie was the name of a dustman, but we didn't care. Freddie it was. It all seemed so futile now.

Finally a woman entered our room and sat down on the end of the bed. She explained that Freddie had been born with a diaphragmatic hernia. Half his diaphragm was missing and all his guts were in his chest. He was now anaesthetised and on full life-support, which meant that a machine was breathing for him, pumping air into his lungs. She gave him a 1 per cent chance of survival and told us we should prepare for him to die. It was a clinical explanation, delivered with little compassion. She had seen it all before and said it all before. She left us alone to grieve.

I felt grief, anger and fear all jumbled together. I wanted to know what 1 per cent meant. Would my baby live or not? And why had everyone missed this on the scans? Had they known and said nothing because it was too late in the day to do anything, or had they really missed it? How could they have missed it? His heart was on the wrong side, his lungs squashed and virtually non-existent, his spleen wedged up under his collarbone, all his intestines and stomach crammed into his chest. I wanted answers, and no one could give me any. Most of all, I wanted to know why God had picked on us yet again. Was it our destiny to be put through continuous agony?

Our families had known that Freddie was to be born that morning. They would have been expecting celebratory calls, and I knew that uncertainty and a sense of dread would now be weighing upon them. I wondered what was going through their minds. Could they have any inkling of the torture we were enduring? I didn't want to weep alone.

Hours had passed, and I still hadn't seen Freddie apart from the few fleeting moments when he was passed over me before being whisked off to the neo-natal ward. Eventually I was wheeled upstairs back to my little room. The empty plastic crib stood in the corner, a tragic reminder of what could have been. I remember a smiling nurse who clearly didn't know what had happened saying, 'Congratulations' as I was wheeled past her. I said coldly, 'What for?' Anger was the only way I knew how to stem the bitter flow of misery that coursed through me.

That evening we were finally taken to see Freddie. There, in a little incubator, was our tiny baby. Wires poked from every available vein. A tube inserted into his lungs was breathing for him – his chest rose and fell in time with the hum of the machine. Endless bleepers sounded. He was fully anaesthetised, and the paediatrician explained that this was the only possible way of saving him. All the other diaphragmatic hernia babies born in the previous four years had died almost immediately, due to the shock of being operated on. This time they were trying a new approach. They hoped that if they could manage to stabilise Freddie and delay operating for a few days he might have a chance of survival.

I couldn't get near Freddie for all the tubes and wires. I wanted to touch this tiny person who had just been put through more hell than we had. It made me weep to think how much pain they had caused him. Henry had been born peacefully to the sound of Mozart; Freddie's birth couldn't have been more different. And I couldn't even hold him.

I looked round the ward at row upon row of incubators lined up, each one containing a tiny heartbeat struggling for life. A nurse stood with her back to us measuring out medication. I glanced down – she was wearing clogs and across the back of the heel was scrawled 'Boo'. I'd been to a convent school with a girl called Boo – could this be the same person? I needed a ray of hope, someone who would show a bit of compassion and not just spout statistics at me. I asked Michael to go over and ask her, but the moment she turned round I recognised her. She grinned across at me and came over. I don't think she said much – she just held my hand.

I wanted Freddie christened straightaway. I needed to focus on something, and finding the priest became an overwhelming must. But no one could find him – he had gone home. I was furious. People don't just die between nine and five. Michael called my sister Cara, who had taken over from Debbie looking after Henry at home. He explained Freddie's condition and said he was not expected to survive. We gave her the grim task of telephoning everyone to let them know. In some rather masochistic way I wanted to see their incredulity; I wanted to share my total horror with the world, perhaps in an attempt to lessen my pain.

Michael went home, and that night passed in a blur. It was one of the loneliest nights of my life. I could hardly move, and the searing, burning pain on my left side nearly made me pass out. I assumed it was psychological pain, because no one had told me that a caesarean could cause pain on this level. It had to be in my mind. A couple of years later a doctor friend told me that the surgeon had probably cut through a nerve during the caesarean – my symptoms, which continued for a long time afterwards, were totally consistent with this.

I couldn't sleep, but I dreaded the dawn. I felt sure my baby lay dead and that someone would arrive at any moment to give me the tragic news. When Michael arrived he too looked grey with lack of sleep. I asked him to telephone the neo-natal ward before we went down: I needed to know that he was still alive before we got there.

Freddie had made it through his first night, and we were free to go and see him at any time.

That day I passed my consultant in the corridor. He licked one finger and held it up in the air, to indicate that Freddie had survived one day. A couple of years later Michael and I heard he had been struck off the medical register for malpractice. Michael's only comment was, 'It couldn't have happened to a nicer guy!' We both wondered whether, if he had bothered to attend even one of my scans, he might have spotted Freddie's problems. Had they known what was wrong they could have given him oxygen the moment he was born, instead of delaying for twenty minutes and almost certainly causing further complications. The priest arrived, and he turned out to be a lovely man with a very sympathetic face and kindly eyes. I knew he'd seen it all before – so many distraught parents and dying children. I asked him why God had done this to us, although I knew and he knew that there was no answer. All he could say was that we would probably never know.

Michael rang four of our close friends and asked them to be godparents. They would be unable to attend, as the ceremony was to take place in a matter of hours, so their role would be done by proxy. How hard it must have been for them to accept such an accolade in such tragic circumstances – a child they would probably never meet. A christening robe was found and draped over Freddie's tubes. The priest, Michael and I stood around him while he was christened. I felt calm. If Freddie was not meant to survive he could go in peace now. I was trying to prepare myself for the inevitable. Only 1 per cent survived, and I didn't feel that lucky.

That afternoon the paediatric surgeon visited us – he was bright, breezy and professional, with a twinkle in his eye, and he gave us our first real ray of hope. He said, 'Your son is a fighter.' He explained that once in a while a baby arrived who he knew was a survivor, and Freddie was one of these babies. He also pointed out that the 1 per cent survival statistic was rubbish – it was all or nothing, and all sounded pretty good. We had to agree.

Boo had kindly made arrangements for a TV monitor to be placed in my room so that I could watch Freddie from my bed. But this turned out to be a nightmare. Every now and then Freddie's tubes would suddenly block, alarms would bleep and twenty staff would run to his side. I never knew what was going on and dreaded these theatrical interludes. When the TV broke I asked them to remove it.

Flowers and letters poured in. I'd never seen so many flowers – dustbins were used instead of vases, and my room began to resemble a florist's shop. No one else on that floor got a look in. I received vast quantities of letters, all expressing the same shock. No one could believe that we had been struck such a cruel blow yet again.

Everyone, but everyone, was praying for Freddie. I remember one friend writing to say she had five hundred nuns praying for him in Calcutta – he must have been one of the most prayed for babies ever. It gave me the courage to dare to hope. I prayed every hour on the hour, I beseeched and pleaded with God. On the ground floor of the hospital was a small chapel. I spent many hours in there, afraid that if I didn't keep up my vigil he would surely die. I became obsessive in my prayer.

The hospital, with its grey walls and endless corridors, became so familiar that I couldn't remember ever being anywhere else. I wasn't eating at all – my days had become a feverish whirl of manic and obsessive prayer. I hadn't put on any weight before the birth, and in the days after it I lost another stone. The relevance of time disappeared, and I felt as if I had ceased to exist in any physical reality. The hours became a monotonous cycle – I was stuck in a time warp of heartbreak and hope. I was able to visit Freddie and the chapel at any time of the day or night – neither the chapel nor the neo-natal ward ever closed. So I went between them, catnapping when my eyes could no longer bear the light.

I tried expressing milk and found it incredibly hard. I had succeeded when I had done it for Henry but now, faced with storing endless filled bottles that might never get used, I found it excruciatingly difficult. One of the nurses told me it would never be wasted as they could always use it for another baby. I gave up that very day. The anguish was too great for me. I wasn't a big enough person to do it for someone else.

On the third day Chris, Henry's lovely physiotherapist, came to visit. She had only just learned of our latest tragedy and was really shocked that this had happened to us – she could hardly meet my eyes. When she saw the empty plastic crib in the corner of the room she looked horrified. She felt it was a cruel reminder of my missing baby and ordered it to be removed. But for me it had become a symbol of hope, and I felt hollow when I came back that afternoon after visiting Freddie to find it gone.

Our son had been born on the Tuesday and christened and confirmed on the Wednesday. Now we were told that he would be operated on the following Monday, if all went well. Depression, self-pity and exhaustion summed up my mental state. Monday morning arrived, and the nurses came to say that Freddie was about to be wheeled into surgery and did I want to go in with him. He was still under general anaesthetic, having been kept unconscious since his birth. I lay there in a heap, certain he wouldn't survive. I didn't want to say a formal goodbye to my baby and let him go to surgery alone.

I prayed all that day while the surgery on my tiny son continued for hour after hour. I wondered how they would manage to reorganise Freddie's insides and put them back as they should have been. I knew his life hung in the balance. It was not just a question of surviving the operation, which was devastating enough at such a tender age; there was also uncertainty about whether Freddie had enough lung capacity. As he grew in the womb his guts had travelled into his chest so that his lungs had been squashed and unable to develop fully. When the surgeon pulled everything out of the chest to allow his lungs to re-expand, would he have enough lung capacity to sustain life? They had explained to us that he might have – in some babies with his condition the guts travel up and down the chest cavity while *in utero*, allowing the lungs to develop more fully. We had no way of knowing which category Freddie would fall into until they operated.

That morning I wandered into the neo-natal ward and was introduced to a distraught father in a little waiting room attached to the ward. His baby girl had been born that morning with a massive diaphragmatic hernia. That was in Brighton, and she had been transferred to London because Great Ormond Street and St George's were the only two hospitals capable of operating on these babies. The mum had been left behind with postnatal problems and needed surgery. Dad was sitting in the ward looking utterly bereft and lost. Like us, he was submerged in a waking nightmare with few details to go on. I sat down and explained that Freddie was in surgery for the same condition and that they had fought to stabilise him for the past week before operating, to give him his best chance of survival. I was sure the same pattern would follow with their baby, and tried to give him courage.

Freddie made it through the operation. That evening he was placed back in the acute nursing section. He had a team who watched his every flicker – this was the NHS at its very best. I sat looking at him. His lungs were just large enough for him to be able to breathe independently – but not yet. For the moment the ventilator breathed for him. He had survived so far. Perhaps I would take my baby home after all. I still hardly dared hope. I might be tempting fate.

As I sat next to Freddie I could see the baby whose father I had talked to earlier being held by her aunt. The father stood by her side. They had taken her off life-support – her lungs were too underdeveloped to ventilate and she was dying. My heart bled for them. Why should my child survive and not theirs? I couldn't face watching their baby die; they had no privacy as their tragedy unfolded before us.

Next to the neo-natal ward were two small, cube-like rooms, decorated in Laura Ashley prints, for parents of acutely sick babies. The idea was that you could be close at hand, and at your baby's side within seconds. We were now given one of these rooms. But we slept very little. Not only were our nerves stretched tight with worry over our tiny son, but we were next to the delivery rooms. The screams of women in labour echoed along the corridors night after night. One night we listened to a particularly vociferous mother-to-be. As the screams drew closer together we knew silence would soon be upon us the moment her baby gulped its first breath of air. But it was a long labour!

Freddie remained on full life-support under general anaesthetic and would do so for the foreseeable future – this was the only way they knew how to stabilise him and give him a chance to recover from the shock of the operation. He had doubled in size from all the drugs pumped into him, and I hardly recognised him. The scar across his stomach stretched out like an angry welt. His abdomen had never grown big enough to house all his guts, and now that they had been re-placed it seemed distorted and bloated. The surgeon had not managed to get Freddie's appendix back in the right place, so rather than placing it on the wrong side they took it out. They had also had great difficulty in extricating his spleen from under his collarbone, but had eventually been successful. Not too much damage had been done.

The days passed by in a strange blur, every day merging seamlessly into the next. By the end of the second week Freddie was beginning to stabilise. I hadn't stepped outside the hospital for two and a half weeks and felt I had become an institutionalised zombie. My clothes reeked of hospital, and the constant bleeping of alarms rang in my head even when there was silence. My mind and my body felt separate from each other, and a surreal detachment set me apart from everyone else.

In all this time, so completely wrapped up in my own misery and Freddie's fate, I had barely thought about Henry at all. Cara had stepped in to care for Henry while Michael was at the hospital with me, and we were hugely grateful. Once Michael was able to go home at night he and Debbie managed between them. I wasn't supposed to drive, but suddenly I needed to see Henry. The day I drove out of St George's it was as if someone had released me from an intense nightmare. The sun shone and people were going about their business, completely oblivious to my agony. For a brief moment it felt so unreal that I wondered if the past few weeks had all been a figment of my imagination. I drove home marvelling at everyday life – even the smell of London was a welcome respite from the chemical odour that had infused my every moment in the hospital.

I arrived home and there was my beautiful bonny Henry. It was so good to have physical contact with real flesh and blood, a sensation that I had so sorely been denied with Freddie. The sterile environment of the hospital seemed a distant and hideous memory. I wandered round Battersea Park, pushing Henry in his buggy. At night I returned to the hospital and to the world of different smells, bleeps and hoping. Until then I hadn't wanted to share my grief – it had felt too overwhelming and I'd needed to grieve alone. But now that a ray of hope had re-entered I needed the encouragement of others, and friends and family began to visit.

It was at this time, while Freddie was still in hospital, that our health visitor suggested we look at schools for Henry. We lived in the London Borough of Wandsworth and there were two primary schools there for children with special educational needs, Greenmead and Paddock. We instantly liked Greenmead and didn't like Paddock. Henry had already been statemented, which involved the Borough Education Department assessing him and producing a statement of his educational needs. Based on this we asked for Henry to go to Greenmead, which clearly suited his needs better. Wandsworth said no. Paddock was the cheaper option and they wanted us to send Henry there. Without an ounce of sympathy for the fact that our second son was on life-support, we were put through the ordeal of getting reports from an array of experts, including Henry's physiotherapist and paediatrician, to support our choice. After which we could only wait and see what Wandsworth decided.

When Freddie was three and a half weeks old the surgeon said he was stable enough for me to hold him. He was still anaesthetised. I sat next to the incubator while a nurse carefully placed him on my lap. This was my first physical contact with him. He was tiny and weighed little more than four pounds. I felt elated and terrified at the same time. I wept to think how much he had already suffered in his short life. He wore a little bonnet with ribbons either side to hold the ventilator tube, which ran into his mouth and down his throat. I had never seen his hair. I assumed he would have lots, like Henry, but when I lifted up the bonnet I discovered it was very short and very dark. That afternoon I felt I got to know Freddie a little bit more, and holding him I was able to begin to bond.

When Freddie was five weeks old they transferred him from the ventilator on to oxygen. He had now been anaesthetised for so long that they were anxious about whether he would actually come round from the anaesthetic. But very slowly he did. Watching him open his eyes for the first time, I wondered whether he remembered the hell he had been through. And if he did, how would it affect him?

My longing to take him home was overwhelming, but the hospital wanted to get his weight up a little higher. So far he'd been fed through a tube going into his stomach via his nose. Now they were suggesting I breastfed him. I felt terrified, as I had little milk left and no confidence at all in breastfeeding. I had failed with Henry and didn't want to fail again. But I agreed to give it a try. I was allowed to take him into my little box-room with me for the night. This was our very first time alone. I tried breastfeeding him on and off through the night, but he didn't make much effort and the next morning when they weighed him he'd lost a gram. I decided to give up and go for the bottle. I would be able to monitor what he was getting with certainty – and God, how I needed a bit of certainty!

A few days later we were told we could take him home. I felt I was being given my life back.

Chapter 5

The first night Freddie spent at home with us he slept in the middle of our bed. I lay there looking at him peacefully asleep, hardly able to believe he was mine at last. I had no wish for sleep, I only wished for this moment of stillness to last for ever. I sent out a silent prayer of thanks.

We settled into a routine. Freddie was still very tiny and his skin had a white-blue tinge to it, but he was feeding well and gaining weight. By six weeks he was smiling. After the loneliness of being with Henry I felt my heart would burst with joy at the eye contact Freddie made and the wonderful gurgles emerging from him. On a visit to Michael's parents I perched Freddie's bouncy chair on the kitchen table and he giggled and giggled at all his little cousins surrounding him. Henry was completely aware of Freddie and had accepted this new addition into our house with no jealousy at all. Freddie loved to hear Henry laugh, and I sensed the beginnings of a bond between the brothers.

A few weeks after Freddie came out of hospital Wandsworth asked me to spend several days at both of Henry's potential schools. I'd just spent the most arduous six weeks of my life at St George's, but despite my exhaustion and stress Wandsworth was implacable and refused to exempt me. It was only after I had spent these required days and after the head teacher of Greenmead, the school of our choice, had given Henry a place that Wandsworth relented and agreed he could go there. They knew we would almost certainly have won at a tribunal, as both schools were within the borough. Years later, while battling over Henry's secondary schooling, we applied under the Data Protection Act for all his notes. There, scribbled in the margin, were the clearly discernible words, 'Yet another family that has won over us on Paddock.'

By three and a half months Freddie was happy and content but he fed greedily and often. I was still incredibly tired. One or both of us had been up every night for the past four years, ever since Henry was born. His limbs became tangled easily and he needed straightening out, as well as frequent nappy changes. Now, with the added task of feeding Freddie several times a night, it was fast becoming too much for either of us to handle.

When we'd first tried baby rice on Henry he'd been deeply offended and had spat it out in disgust. It had taken some cajoling to get him to swallow any of it. Freddie couldn't have been more different. He loved it, grinned with satisfaction and immediately slept through the night.

The next night we gave him baby rice again. All seemed well until the last mouthful, when Freddie coughed and the entire bowlful re-emerged in a funnel that shot six feet across the room and landed in the middle of a rather tatty Persian rug. Both of us sat in stunned silence; we had never seen anything like it before.

Freddie didn't bat an eyelid – it was if nothing had happened at all. After a moment or two we laughed – it was truly one of the funniest sights we'd ever seen. We decided to feed him again but gave him less. This time we had success, and Freddie settled down for the night.

Over the next few days we learned that if we fed Freddie just one spoonful too much we'd get the entire contents back across the room. We had to get the quantity just right to avoid these messy torpedoes. Freddie never seemed at all upset when his meal re-emerged in such an abrupt fashion, and gradually we learned to get the portion size right. Because he seemed so calm about it and ate if we gave him small portions, at first we didn't think anything was wrong. But gradually his vomiting became more frequent. By this time he wasn't just vomiting at mealtimes: if anyone annoyed him he'd cough and this would be followed by a large funnel of puke, usually aimed in the direction of the culprit. One day a friend came to visit and brought a couple of teddies for the boys. Henry happily chewed his, but Freddie took one look at the teddy being held out to him and puked. Our guest couldn't quite believe that offering the teddy had resulted in such a clear 'get lost'. The teddy was offered again and Freddie, his eye firmly fixed on the offending object, puked again, leaving our friend stunned with disbelief. No one could believe Freddie's ability to send a jet of vomit up to fifteen feet across a room until they saw it for themselves.

Henry too was vomiting. He was so floppy he was a bit like a hot water bottle – every time he bent over or squished sideways he'd spout a mouthful of puke. It stank, so he was immediately changed. He could go through eight, nine or ten outfits per day, and so could Freddie. I could hardly cope with the laundry. Six loads a day was normal and, although we did have a washing machine, we had no dryer. Thankfully, Michael's mum came to the rescue and installed one for us. Despite this, coping with the vast quantities of puke-soaked clothes still took hours each day and was rapidly becoming a nightmare. And it wasn't just the endless clothes – the boys were vomiting over curtains, sofa covers and carpets. Our house looked like a public laundry, with damp washing covering every available surface.

By the time Freddie was eight months old we knew we needed help and we decided to take him back to the hospital. Since he came home we'd had no follow-up of any kind – no one had called to see how he was getting on or asked us to bring him back for a check-up. But not only was he vomiting frequently, he was also very small, because it was difficult to get him to keep any food down. Surely his problems must relate to the diaphragmatic hernia?

Back at St George's Hospital we sat nervously in the waiting room. I didn't like being back – it made me feel thoroughly on edge and very snappy. When we were eventually called in we found ourselves seated in front of the same woman paediatrician who had coldly and clinically given us Freddie's diagnosis in the first awful hours following his birth. I felt a sense of foreboding.

She suggested we try a combination of drugs which would help to get the food through Freddie's gut slightly more quickly and, she hoped, help him keep it on board.

No technical explanations for his condition were given. When the paediatrician started to do some developmental tests on Freddie I froze – I'd been through all that with Henry and had never really got over the shock of seeing the hopeless look in the doctor's eyes. It doesn't take much to work out what they're thinking, and I dreaded being exposed to that again. I wanted to hold Freddie tightly to me and say, 'Hey, we only brought him to you to discuss his puking. Nothing else, thanks.' But she was oblivious and proceeded to offer Freddie little bricks, which she said he ought to be stacking. He showed no interest other than throwing them on the floor. She then offered him a book, pointing out that he ought to be turning the pages by now. My heart sank – I'd never really noticed whether he could actually turn pages. He was so far ahead of Henry that any skills he possessed seemed thoroughly miraculous to us.

Freddie obligingly took the book, looked at it and did turn a handful of pages at a time. She looked doubtful and, perhaps simultaneously, became aware of our nervous looks. Brusquely she suggested we try the medication, book in to see the dietician and bring him back if the problem continued. The hospital had also suggested we ring our health visitor and ask for some help with the boys. We had Debbie, our nanny, but laundry was not in her job description.

We started the medication and it worked. We were so relieved. But our relief was short-lived – within a week Freddie had worked out the timing of the doses and could puke before it took effect. We tried everything to keep his food inside him. Sometimes it worked, sometimes it didn't. He continued to belch out small mouth-fuls of food, which meant just as many changes of clothes as Henry, if not more.

I called our health visitor, who came and assessed us and delved deep into our personal lives. She agreed we needed help and contacted social services. Neither of us fancied the stigma attached to telling social services we couldn't cope, but at this stage we had no choice because we were getting desperate. A social worker came and assessed us, agreed we had a big problem and assured us we would get help. I was thrilled – the laundry was crippling and any help with it would be a real bonus.

A few weeks later we received a call saying we could have eight hours of help with the laundry. I was over the moon. This would lift a heavy burden – I thought they'd only offer us three or four hours per week. I thanked them profusely. There was a silence down the phone – it wasn't eight hours per week, it was eight hours per year. I didn't know whether to laugh or cry. But, determined to be grateful for this pitiful amount of help, I booked the social services-approved laundry lady to come the fol-lowing Saturday for our first four hours of help. We had a hospital appointment and had to leave shortly after she arrived. She asked us to sign her chitty, and in return we asked if she could put the keys through the front door once she'd finished. On our return from the hospital we discovered she must have taken off the moment we walked out of the door. Not a single item of laundry had been done. I didn't bother asking for the second four hours.

We now had one severely disabled child and another

with ongoing major health problems. Social services had acknowledged that we were a family with a high level of needs, yet when I didn't claim our second laundry session they closed our file. We plainly didn't need any help and they were happy to walk away.

Debbie had now been with us for nearly four years and was twenty-one – it was time for her to move on. We advertised in *Tomorrow's News Today* and the *Lady* for an Australian or New Zealand girl. They had a reputation for being good carers, and we wanted someone lively and fun.

Endless people rang about the job, but when I described it no one wanted it. I knew I couldn't cope alone, and as the time drew near for Debbie to leave I was becoming increasingly desperate. Just as complete panic was about to set in, a girl with a very strong accent rang. Her English was pretty awful and she told us she was Hungarian. She sounded keen, even when I went into great detail about the boys, puking and all, so we invited her round and we all sat rather nervously on the edge of the sofa. The boys were in bed upstairs and she immediately wanted to see them. Freddie was still awake in his cot, happily playing with toys, so I brought him down. She immediately sat him on her lap and engaged with him. She radiated warmth. We'd found our girl.

Her name was Angela, she was twenty and we happily gave her the job. After her first few weeks with us we all agreed that it was going incredibly well. Angela adored the boys and they adored her. I too had found a friend, and we soon established a real sense of companionship. Over the years Angela was to become one of my staunchest allies. I could never have survived if it had not been for her wonderful, intelligent support and friendship.

A few weeks later we moved house. We had outgrown our little two-up, two-down and desperately needed more space. The house we found was not far away and had been on the market for ages. When we were shown around we soon realised why. The olive green drawing room with the lime green ceiling and avocado cornicing was complemented by flock wallpaper and multi-patterned carpets. The entire house appeared to have been decorated by people suffering from severe visual impairment or else high on drugs. We got it for a bargain price and I spent the next two years redecorating it.

When the summer arrived I was longing to take off and have a holiday for a couple of weeks. I asked my mother whether she and my stepfather and Tilly, now aged sixteen, wanted to split the cost of renting a farmhouse in the Loire Valley in France. They were delighted. Although my mother and stepfather had by now been divorced for some years they still, rather eccentrically, regularly spent holidays together. I set about booking a house and asked Angela whether she would need a visa. At which point she shuffled from foot to foot and looked mortified before blurting out that in fact she was Yugoslav, had lost her passport and was not able to renew it because of the war in the Balkans. She hadn't told us that she was Yugoslav as we might have been prejudiced, and anyway she was in fact half Hungarian. I wanted to explode. At the interview we had specifically discussed travelling with us on holiday. She had known she wouldn't get the job if she told the truth, and had just hoped we wouldn't go on holiday too soon.

The risk she'd taken had paid off. Once I calmed down I realised that girls like this didn't present themselves too often. Her relationship with the boys outweighed any misdemeanour and, besides, I liked her enormously. I talked to Michael and we decided to call Debbie and see if she could come on holiday with us. She immediately said yes. Problem solved. Everyone was happy.

The holiday was a partial success. The trouble was that everyone wanted to relax and do as little as possible, but with two small needy children this was an impossibility and the atmosphere became rather fraught. There was one real bonus, though. The farm had lots of rather tatty chickens milling around. As it was so hot we left all the doors open and the chickens wandered into the vast kitchen looking for crumbs. So each time Freddie puked we had our automatic vacuum cleaners to assist with the mess.

We came back and settled into a routine. Henry, now four and a half, started at Greenmead in September. We were offered the school bus, but I was far too attached to Henry and drove him in myself. I was supposed to go with him only for the first few days, to settle him in, but I ended up staying for the year. The school was fabulous and the teachers warm and welcoming. While I was at school with Henry Angela looked after Freddie, and the arrangement worked well for all of us.

Soon after Henry started there, the head of Greenmead told me they had been trying to get funding for a hydrotherapy swimming pool. Wandsworth had agreed to provide half the cost if the school could raise the rest. They needed £60,000, and so far they'd had very little success. I immediately saw this as a challenge and offered to have a bash at raising the money. I rang various charities and told them that others had promised donations and that their generous donation, should they feel inclined to give, would complete the amount needed to allow these deprived children to have their much-needed pool. It worked, and within six weeks I'd got the money. Michael and I were invited to Wandsworth town hall for a celebratory drink with Alf Dubbs, now Lord Dubbs, formerly Labour MP for Battersea.

Raising the money for the pool gave me my first experience of what was possible with a little determination and effort. Later, when I went on to set up my own charity, I knew, because of this, that I could do it.

Two weeks after I'd given birth to Freddie, Sally, the girlfriend I'd been away with when we were both pregnant, had produced a boy named Thomas. I hadn't seen her during the summer break and now she popped over for tea with Molly and Thomas. I couldn't believe how big and sturdy her son was – he was a little younger than Freddie, but far bigger. My heart sank when I saw him walking – he was only ten months old and charging all over the place, while Freddie was still only sitting. Thomas was also saying lots of words, 'hoover' being his latest; Freddie was saying nothing.

I smiled, but inside I was screaming – this couldn't be happening again. I remembered the look of concern on the paediatrician's face. Was I pulling the wool over my own eyes? Did Freddie have more than just his surgical problems? I felt I was quietly dying inside. There had to be another reason that Freddie was so behind.

We started making up excuses for Freddie. Everyone did – no one wanted to see us go through more agony. But as time went by, and we watched other children, it became apparent that all was not well. I wanted to hide away from the world. I had come to terms with Henry's problems but didn't feel I could share this new pain with anyone. I quietly withdrew, feeling unable to cope. My sister-in-law had become pregnant three months after me. Her son Tom was one of those babies who bounced and gurgled and did all the right things well ahead of time. I couldn't face the family gatherings any more. I felt ashamed, embarrassed, humiliated and afraid.

When he was about eighteen months old we decided to send Freddie to the same small council-run special needs nursery which Henry had attended for a while. It was scruffy and desperately under-funded, but the atmosphere was warm and only a handful of children attended, which we felt might be good for Freddie. We used the excuse that he was fragile, rather than disabled – we simply couldn't face the possibility that his delayed development might be anything other than temporary. The two women running the nursery, however, made it perfectly clear, without a hint of sensitivity, that they thought Freddie was autistic and disabled. I couldn't bear to hear this and removed him. From then on we sent him, with Angela, to a private nursery where we could avoid the hurt of cruel, uninvited comments.

One evening Sally called me to say they'd found a wonderful new healer and psychic in Kensington, who she felt was really helping Molly. Sally thought I should go along. But we had become rather cynical about healers. When Lilly had been doing a session with Henry she had suddenly announced that he would be healed, and that she could do it within twelve weeks. Michael and I were somewhat sceptical, but naturally we desperately wanted it to be true. Twelve weeks later there was absolutely no change in Henry.

With a fair amount of trepidation I telephoned and made an appointment with this new healer, Keith. I went alone to check him out before bringing the boys. He was about thirty-five and totally bald and said I could take notes on what he said but I couldn't tape it as the radio waves would interfere with him and he wouldn't be able to transmit properly. I wanted to laugh – it sounded like rubbish to me. He sat in silence and then inhaled and exhaled. I felt daft. Then he suddenly started holding his stomach and clutching his throat. I was there on behalf of Henry and immediately said no, not this. Keith was discussing Freddie and I didn't want to know. I was still telling myself that Freddie would be fine – I wasn't prepared to listen to the possibility of anything being seriously wrong with him.

Keith switched to Henry and began talking to Henry's 'higher self'. I didn't know what to make of this – Henry was asleep in Battersea. My spiritual knowledge was sorely lacking and it seemed like hocus-pocus to me. But Keith said that Henry was not in his body. He told me that my son's attempts to enter his body were jarring; something was preventing him from being fully in his body, but Henry knew he would have to come 'down' one day, and he would. Keith was talking in a totally new way. It wasn't the kind of language I understood, but it fitted with what our first medium had said – that Henry would grow out of it. I longed to believe these mediums, but I was finding it hard. Henry couldn't even sit and still didn't have much head control; it was going to take a miracle to make their predictions come true.

I went over and over this strange meeting in my mind. What did it all mean? I had sat and pondered for many hours over why God should have given me two such lovely but complicated children. I felt certain that there was a good reason for all that had happened to us. My own early vision of Henry standing, fit and well, in a library, and the visions of the mediums, added to my conviction that I was on some strange but unknown journey with a very definite purpose.

I decided to go back to see Keith, but found that he'd left. The receptionist suggested I saw someone else – a 'nice chap called David' happened to be free that very afternoon. Since I felt I had nothing to lose, I decided to see him. There were so many questions I wanted to ask. Would another medium give the same prognosis for Henry? Would he confirm that I was on a path towards some as yet unknown purpose?

I met David at the reception desk and followed him upstairs. He suffered from cerebral palsy which had left him hemiplegic and only able to walk very slowly with the aid of a stick. We mounted the stairs at snail's pace and chatted, nervously on my part, on the way up. I guessed he was from Iraq or Iran, and said I restored Islamic manuscripts. He immediately told me to say nothing about myself, as he would be able to give a far better picture if he began with a blank screen. When we sat down together David talked of me being in a gilded prison – not unhappy, but with no freedom. He said I was a warrior for my children. He also said that Henry's journey would take a few years, but that I would find the answer to his condition and he would be healed. I left feeling certain that my journey had begun, although I had no idea where to start. I decided I would try anything and anyone who came my way.

In the meantime I still had to cope with the tremendous task of caring for both boys, which was becoming increasingly demanding as the months went by. Angela remained as loyal and hard-working as ever, but even with her help it was exhausting. Michael was working long hours and would muck in when he got home. By the time the boys were in bed both of us would be on our knees. Henry was still having fits, often as many as thirty a day. They were often triggered by certain textures or sounds. He was hugely sensitive, as if every sensation he felt was multiplied by a thousand and caused him great distress. We were continually having to find ways to make his life more comfortable. We learned never to switch the vacuum cleaner on near him or to play the wrong music; if we did, he would start howling. He hated any form of breeze and had to be covered by a plastic awning on his buggy or he'd whinge all the time. He also hated the feel of grass, sand and fibrous materials.

He could be incredibly wilful when he wanted, as I discovered when I decided to take him to *Swan Lake* at the Royal Opera House. He had always loved the music and so we set off for our treat, leaving Freddie with Michael. At the theatre I sat Henry firmly on my lap, which placed him neatly above the head of the woman sitting in front. Henry had a thing about hair, and if someone's head was in range he would immediately and very determinedly pull it. The lady in front of us had a particularly bouffant hairdo – all too tempting for Henry to sink his little hands into. I was forced to clamp them firmly into his lap and keep tight hold of them through-out the performance. Towards the end of the final act this restriction was beginning to enrage Henry, normally a very passive little boy, and he turned his head towards me and bit me hard on the shoulder. I could feel the blood dribbling down inside my shirt. I was so angry that I removed him from the last act and plonked him in the corridor.

Freddie too was a real handful. Although his medica-tion ensured that a reasonable amount of what he ate stayed inside him, he was still projectile vomiting several times a day, over whoever happened to be standing next to him. He was sitting and cheerful, but there was still no sign of him walking or talking. He did make some progress, though. Between the ages of nine months and a year he began to feed himself little pots of yogurt, holding the pot in one hand and dipping the spoon with the other. We felt hopeful.

But by the age of two Freddie was still not walking. We made up the excuse that it was due to nerve damage from his operation. In addition, he didn't say a word and had lost some of his earlier skills. He had stopped feeding himself soon after his first birthday, and it was as if he had withdrawn. To us, it appeared as though he was absorbing Henry's lack of ability and deciding to be like him.

At the same time he became very frustrated and started banging his head against whatever object was near enough. He would bang so hard that it virtually drew blood and we'd all come running. Between the puking on demand and the head-banging he managed to keep us in almost constant attendance, and it became very frustrating. We felt he was manipulating us and demanding attention, but what we didn't know at the time was that he was in severe pain. Only later did we learn that the valve to his stomach did not shut properly, and the constant searing pain of severe acid reflux encouraged Freddie to vomit to relieve the burning sensation and the build-up of acid in his throat. Years later, when his condition became acute and needed surgical intervention, the surgeon told us that the level of pain Freddie must have suffered would have brought a grown man to his knees.

As the months went by he became more and more withdrawn and more and more frustrated. He used to pick up stones and rub them on his legs almost as if he was trying to feel them. It was if his legs were numb. Neither of us knew what to do, and no one else knew what to say to us. I began to think Freddie might be deaf, since his hearing seemed to be so selective. Sometimes he heard us; at other times he would appear completely deaf. We decided to get his hearing checked.

My friend Sally had recommended a lovely specialist they had seen for Molly at a private clinic. We booked an appointment. The specialist was German and had a gentle and efficient manner. She looked as though she knew her stuff. We sat Freddie on the floor and she moved round him, testing him with various sounds. He did seem to look up at the appropriate moments, but I could see she wasn't totally sure about him. After a while she sat back and said she thought his hearing was within the normal range. We asked her about his lack of speech and his frustrated behaviour. She sat back, a pensive look on her face. She appeared to be trying to find the right words. Very gently she suggested we might want to see a developmental specialist.

I felt my world was falling apart.

Chapter 6

The thought of seeing the specialist forced us to take off the blinkers we'd hung on to for so long. We had to admit that Freddie, too, was disabled and it hit us hard. How on earth do you accept that lightning has struck twice? Distraught didn't come close to what we felt. It was too cruel, too unjust to bear.

But perhaps there was relief, too. We had fought against accepting that there was anything wrong with Freddie for far too long. Now it was time to face up to it. Why should this have happened? No one knew, but I felt that, despite the heartache involved, this was in some strange way a gift. What a great compliment, to be given two such incredible children. It might seem strange, but I felt that at some level I had chosen this and that perhaps my children had chosen this path too, and we had come together to achieve something.

Sometimes I found it hard to reconcile the two aspects of myself. On one hand I was simply a mum dealing with all the hard work and raw emotions that came with two severely disabled children. On the other I believed deeply that this was meant to be and that we were on a path together. The trouble is, it's one thing believing something and another altogether having to live the belief day in and day out. For all my efforts, there were moments when I just longed for the ordinary, the normal and the mundane.

Faced with Freddie's emerging disabilities, Michael and I once again considered the possibility of putting our boys into care – a suggestion made to us by several people. We knew that they meant well and were concerned for us, but we also knew that for us it was simply not an option. We didn't love our children any less than the parents of able children did. Why would we give them up simply because they presented us with more challenges? If a normal child had an accident and became disabled as a result, would their parents love them less, or want them less? To us it was simple – our boys were ours and always would be.

Caring for the boys took up most of my time. I worked with Angela and was so grateful for her company because, truth to tell, our endless and repetitive routine was often mind-numbingly boring. I felt guilty about it, but repeating the same actions over and over again with no prospect of anything different was my worst nightmare and my biggest challenge. I longed for more from the boys – smiles, chatter, laughter, games we could play together. I often felt very lonely as I plodded through chore after chore, day after day.

I would get up in the morning knowing that Henry would have been sick in the night, which meant I had to change his sheets every day. Freddie would often spread poo around his bed, which meant changing his sheets too. The boys had to be washed, dressed and fed, and this could take a couple of hours before we set about the rest of our day.

I always looked for interesting and exciting things for us to do. We'd go to galleries, concerts, zoos and museums in an effort to stimulate and interest the boys. Getting around was hard work. I applied to social services for a double buggy, but as Freddie was under five and Henry over five they came under different departments which refused to fund the buggy jointly, so we were turned down. My sister then bought us a wonderful Silver Cross double buggy, with one seat in front of the other. At first this was marvellous, but within a year I couldn't push the front wheels up on to the kerb – the boys' joint weight was just too much for me. Eventually, when Freddie reached five, we were given a side-by-side double buggy by social services; but it was so wide that it wouldn't go through most shop doorways.

I couldn't leave the house with both boys on my own, and this made me feel very trapped. Without someone else to help me load them in and out of cars and buggies I was stuck. I hated this, just as I hated the exhaustion which never left me. I used to dream of being knocked out by a general anaesthetic for a week, so that I could wake up feeling truly rested. I hated the fact that by the time the boys were tucked up in bed I was too tired to read a book and simply slumped in front of the TV. Michael and I were seldom able to do anything that really interested us, and and at times we found this really hard. There were so many things we'd have loved to do. Both of us were adventurous and enjoyed travel, but a rare trip to the cinema was about as far as we were able to go.

For a while we were able to go on holiday at my aunt

and uncle's wonderful Georgian pile in Norfolk, surrounded by acres of stunning countryside. They had
many cottages on the estate and had given each of their
offspring a house. We used to be allowed to rent, fairly
cheaply, one of the cottages that backed on to the Broads
– wonderful lakes that we could boat and fish on. Angela
and I used to take the boys there for the odd week. We
had a blissful time pottering about, taking the boys to
beaches and going boating – it was real time out.

Then suddenly the rent was raised to £30 a day. This
was a lot of money to us – we had two kids with major
problems and far greater expenses than families with
regular kids. My aunt said she'd had to put the rent up to
cover the cost of the electricity. In a fit of pique I turned
the heating full on, opened all the windows and went out
for the day. I always had a vivid imagination and loved
inventing extremely naughty revenges. As children we
had stayed with my aunt and uncle on their estate and
one day, when I felt my aunt was being rather high-
handed, I headed for their stunning walled garden. It was
opened to the public once a year, and behind the exquisite border grew a very old and well-established peach
tree. It took me about three hours to work my way along
it, taking a single bite out of every unripe peach which I
then spat out. I was never found out – I imagine they
must have thought they had an awful infestation from
some large-toothed bug.

Despite what was at times an uncomfortable relationship between my mother and me, she and Freddie had a
very special bond which had begun as soon as he was
born. She had never had this with Henry, but Freddie

was different – there was an undeniable link between them and they adored each other.

My mother had trained as a speech therapist in her forties, but had never practised. A few years later she trained as a primary school teacher and went to work in a small Catholic primary school in Maida Vale called St Joseph's. She loved it, and turned out to be fantastic with small children. When Freddie was four we decided to send him to the nursery class which my mother taught in St Joseph's. Although the school was for mainstream children, the head teacher gladly accepted Freddie and he and my mother were delighted. Freddie was to stay in the nursery class, always with the support of our nanny, until he was seven – way too long, but he was very happy there with my mother, and the head teacher understood and allowed us a free rein. I thank him to this day for showing such compassion.

We continued to see the psychic, David, who gave the boys healing and encouraged me to think in new and broader ways. It was as if he was bringing me out of myself. We had long discussions in which he would quietly, and with great humour and gentleness, challenge my limited and fearful way of thinking. As a Catholic I felt guilty, and always lurking in the background was the horrible feeling that somehow I was being punished. This terrible feeling completely contradicted my sense that the children were in fact an incredible gift. Reconciling the two was tough – old habits die hard. David persuaded me that it was time to adopt more positive and spiritual ways of seeing things and to start to think more creatively.

I had a huge amount of energy and instinctively

wanted to channel it. My past three years had been spent in a state of shock and dealing with immeasurable quantities of grief. There were times when I never thought I would leave those feelings behind, but somehow David gave me back my ability to dream and helped me to believe that I could move on. He encouraged me to see that the next stage was to manifest a path that would honour my children, Michael and myself and all that we had been through. He would tell me that it was a done deal and that I would succeed, and, hearing this, my confidence grew. I felt that, if success was 'written' in this way, all I had to do was simply take each step as it was offered to me.

David was gently introducing the idea of spiritual guides, spiritual family circles and God helping me. At the same time, Michael's mother, Lamorna, sent me a wonderful book called *A Soul's Journey*. It was about a young man who had lost his brother in the war and was taken on a journey through the realms of spirit. The message of the book was that in the physical realm we inhabit we are far from alone. I began to feel the truth of this and to believe that perhaps I could kick some ass up above and get some help. After all, the Bible does say, 'Ask and you shall receive, knock and the door will be opened.' Well, I sure as hell was planning to do a lot of asking and knocking.

A phrase David used the whole time was 'Don't limit yourself.' I began to see that I would express a wish or hope and then immediately put an obstacle in its path, or think of a good reason why it wouldn't happen or why something would stop me. David showed me that the fear within me was one of my greatest hindrances. It was holding me back, but David continued to gently urge me forward. He would say, 'All you'll get from sitting on the fence is a sore bum. Get off the fence and start living.'

I began to realise how incredibly afraid of life I was, and that the fear of living was ingrained deep within me. It was not that I had cultivated such a view of life; it seemed to have developed unconsciously over the years, perhaps in part as a result of the beliefs I was given and the experiences I had had as a child. Now that I could see my own inhibitions, it was a lot easier to go forward with courage. But I was amazed at how much effort it took to find the courage to do new things. Gradually, though, I began to believe in myself, bolstered by the inner knowledge that I was not alone and had support from above. I felt I had no excuse not to get on with following my new path, wherever it took me.

Through St George's I had by now met many parents of disabled children, all on a desperate crusade to find help. The common theme was a feeling of terrible isolation and a complete lack of information across the board, particularly medical information, both conventional and complementary. Gradually the idea of founding a charity to help these parents began to emerge. Angela and I would go into great and lengthy discussions about what the charity should be called and exactly what it would offer.

At this stage it seemed a complete fantasy and I never really believed I was capable of getting the idea off the ground, let alone running it. But as the months passed, and my inner faith that the boys would be well grew stronger, I found that I needed and wanted to set up this charity I was dreaming of. One morning I rang David and asked him how on earth I should start. I didn't know how to coordinate my thoughts into something coherent. David told me to go and get a pen and a sheet of paper and start writing. So I did. I began by asking myself, 'What are the three areas that parents need most help with?' That one was easy: loneliness, information and research. I wrote them down.

For loneliness I wanted centres where parents could bring their disabled children and be surrounded by the facilities and activities that would meet their child's needs. And, most importantly, they would have access to other like-minded parents. Next I wanted a resource centre that parents could ring to get information about who and what might help their child on both the conventional and the complementary medical fronts. I wanted to be able to send out free and comprehensive fact sheets on all types of complementary therapies. Thirdly, I wanted to initiate research projects that would help to find treatments for a range of disabilities.

I rang David back and told him about my ideas. He said it was great and I should go for it. So did Michael. And so the seeds of the Henry Spink Foundation were planted. I wanted to name it after Henry for two reasons. First, because the whole concept of the charity came to me through him, and second, because I felt he was at peace with his disability and would not mind his name being used for such a cause. Freddie was different. I knew he wasn't at ease with his condition and I didn't want him to grow up with a disability label which might make him uncomfortable in the future. But his contribution was just as great. It was Freddie whose suffering gave me the wake-up call to get out there and do something.

Michael and I had recently had supper with my aunt Maggie, my father's youngest sister. My father only saw her very occasionally on his rare visits to England because Maggie and my stepmother, Ann, loathed each other.

We raised the subject of starting up the Henry Spink Foundation. We knew we needed to register the details with the Charity Commissioners, but didn't know where to start. Maggie suggested that we see her solicitor and very kindly offered to pay the £1,000 necessary to set the charity up. In return we suggested that she join us as one of the Trustees of the Foundation. We discussed the structure of the charity, and decided that we needed high-profile people to be involved, in order to lend credibility and weight to the charity and give us a kick-start in raising money. Initially we thought we would approach members of my family. My dad's side was stuffed with aristocrats and I thought I would ask some of them to lend their names to a worthy cause and help get us off the ground. My great-uncle and great-aunt, the Duke and Duchess of Sutherland, seemed a good place to start.

One particular ancestor had increased the family fortunes enormously. Francis Egerton, who was the third Duke of Bridgewater, known as the 'Canal Duke', inherited his title at the age of eleven. He had an unhappy engagement to the beautiful Elizabeth Gunning, which was broken off, and to distract himself he focused on his vast estates which were rich in coal, the richest being Worsley. This was at the beginning of the Industrial Revolution, and the Duke and his agent at Worsley, John Gilbert, decided to build a canal from Worsley to Manchester and Salford in order to carry their coal to these expanding markets. James Brindley was appointed as engineer for the project. An Act of Parliament was necessary before work could start. The first Bridgewater Canal Act was passed in 1759, and the canal reached as far as Manchester in 1764. It was extended to Runcorn in 1776, linking Manchester with the Mersey estuary. The Duke died in 1803 and was buried at Little Gaddesden, near Ashridge in Hertfordshire, having made a significant contribution to the development of industry in England. Another legacy, still to be seen at the Royal Scottish Museum in Edinburgh, was his acquisition of the famous Orleans Collection of over three hundred Italian paintings, which included works formerly owned by many of the royal heads of Europe. These paintings still belong to the Duke of Sutherland and are merely on loan to the museum, and today the family's wealth is estimated to be £250 million.

The Sutherlands, great-uncle John and great-aunt Evelyn, both agreed to join the council of the charity. I also asked another great-aunt, Lady Margaret Colville. Meg had been lady-in-waiting to the Queen Mother for many years. Her late husband, John Colville, known as Jock, had been Principal Private Secretary to Winston Churchill and later equerry to the Queen. Their daughter Harriet had married a Bowes-Lyon, a member of the Queen Mother's family, and was now lady-in-waiting to

Princess Anne. Meg and Harriet both agreed to come on board. I was delighted, I had my bit of old England which I hoped would impress the Americans whose money I was keen to attract – the Americans, with their greater tax incentives, being far more generous than the Brits when it comes to charitable giving.

Next, I needed some celebrities. I knew Trudie Styler had visited Spink and Son, Michael's firm. I wrote and asked her to join the council, and she said yes. I felt I was on a roll.

Now I needed a Patron. Who could I get who was British, popular and well known by young and old? Felicity Kendal popped into my mind. Perfect, I thought – loved by women, adored by men and known by all. I had no idea how to trace her, let alone get a letter to her. But after a bit of digging I found out that there was an agency in central London which listed all the stars' agents. I decided to ring and, much to my astonishment, they readily gave me the name and address of Felicity's agent. It all seemed too easy.

I wrote her a letter which was probably full of hideous spelling mistakes. I had no idea how to use a computer in those days, and spelling had always been my weak point at school. In fact my greatest incentive for learning the ins and outs of computing was the bliss of Spellcheck! Amazingly, Felicity got my letter and immediately agreed to be Patron of the Henry Spink Foundation. I couldn't believe my luck.

This was the beginning of an extraordinary realisation that I could get a positive response from almost anyone in the public eye (with the surprising exception of politicians!), and my confidence was boosted. In later years I was asked whether I had just pulled all the celebrities who joined the Foundation out of my address book. But with the exception of my family, I wrote to everyone as a complete stranger.

I had the beginnings of a structure for the Foundation. Now we needed letterhead, a logo and an image to tell people what the charity was about. We also had to start thinking about offices and staff, and preparing fact-sheets. The first of these needed to be on what the Foundation was going to do. All of these things were outside my experience as a bookbinder; but, amazingly, people came forward to help. A university friend of my sister's, Jenny Hunt, worked for Christie's. She offered to help design the letterhead and Christie's did the printing. She also helped write out the aims of the charity in a form that I could send out to people to raise money and get us going.

At this stage everything was being done from our dining room table, as we had no resources for an office. But we decided that the first aim of the charity would be the resource centre to give out information. This would require an office, computers and staff.

My new-found creativity and energy helped me to live with the grief I had felt for so many years. It was if I was emerging from some horrible dark tunnel. I felt incredibly excited and energised, and wanted to tell the whole world about my new way of thinking. But not everyone was ready for it. I made the mistake of sharing my new exploratory thoughts with my mother, who was still deeply Catholic. She had been brought up, as had many of her generation, in fear of God. I had begun to feel that the fear of God was something used by the Catholic Church to disempower people and stifle any form of creativity. It left people afraid of doing anything that might earn them eternal damnation. My mother became terrified that I was questioning the rules of our faith and introducing elements that might put her faith in doubt. She was afraid that I was consorting with the dead, when in fact all I was doing was acknowledging a world beyond the purely physical and praying for guidance and help.

We had many arguments and never got close to finding a compromise or resolving our differences of opinion. Then one day my mother called to say that she had found a wonderful centre that would do healing on the children. I was extremely surprised at such an invitation. But even if it was a traditional hands-on healing from the Church I was game to go along, particularly if it was going to appease my mother's anger at my new way of thinking.

Angela and I drove, with the boys, to the address that my mother had given us. We arrived early and were shown up some steep stairs. Carrying a boy each, we were taken into a spacious Victorian room. The décor oozed money. This was not at all what I had been expecting. I had thought we were going to be taken to something more traditionally religious such as a chapel.

My mother finally arrived, and shortly afterwards a strange-looking woman entered the room. She was about sixty-five and reminded me of a nun, though she wore no habit. Her hair was in black and white streaks and she had jet-black eyes. I had Henry on my lap, while Angela was on the other side of the room with Freddie. The woman seated herself in front of me and, without any preamble, accused me of consorting with the dead. Startled, I pointed out that St Christopher was a man who had been given sainthood and that Catholics now prayed to him in spirit for safety, which was surely also a form of consorting with the dead. She snapped back that it was not relevant and that he had been struck off anyway. The next moment she stood up and started waving an imaginary sword about, pretending that she was cutting the evil from me and the boys. We were being exorcised.

I was about to get up and leave when I caught Angela's eye. She was laughing. I stayed where I was and the exorcism continued while Angela and I tried not to catch each other's eye and laugh. Thank God the boys were completely oblivious to what was going on. Henry, indeed, was fast asleep.

When it was all over we walked down the stairs and I saw my mother give £100 to someone at the bottom. I turned to the woman, who was standing behind us, and said, 'If you take a single penny from my mother ever again, I will go to the press.' After this I don't think I spoke to my mother for several months. Funny it may have been, but it was hurtful too, and it was a while before I was able to forgive her.

While I was working with David and learning about positive thinking I was also exploring the conventional medical path. Great Ormond Street had essentially told us to go away and didn't have any further answers to

Henry's condition. But something was nagging in the back of my mind. I didn't know why, but every fibre in my body told me to start reading again – biology, neurology and biochemistry. I devoured everything in sight and I began to ask questions. I had this crazy thought that a pollutant, possibly a metal, was preventing my child's brain from functioning normally. I had no proof at all, only a mother's gut instinct – which is worth absolutely zero in the medical establishment.

At this stage I concentrated on Henry because we had been left with no answers about his condition. Here was a child of seven with no brain damage who behaved like a brain-damaged person. Freddie's condition was easier to understand, and though we still didn't have all the answers for him either, I felt that the first step was to try to unlock the secret of Henry's brain.

I knew I wanted to see a biochemist rather than a neurologist. Neurology is a bit like having a mechanic look at the car engine to find the fault. But this had been tried, and no one had come up with anything structurally wrong with Henry's mechanics. Now I wanted someone who could look at the make-up of the fuel which ran the car. Michael's father had mentioned some time before that he knew a biochemist called John McLaren Howard. He had a private practice, but I decided this might be good. If I was paying he might at least listen to my ideas and not just chuck me out for wasting his time.

When I arrived at John's office I felt like an uneducated idiot, and was sure he'd laugh at me. But he didn't. He watched Henry and listened patiently as I explained my theory. When I'd finished, John pondered and scratched his head. Then he said quietly that he thought I might just be right.

I had spent the past three years since Henry's MRI scan in a complete void, with no one to turn to. Now this man in front of me appeared to be agreeing with my ideas. Not only that, but he said he would take Henry on as a research case and not charge me. I sat there in disbelief. He knew that the level of work involved in finding a pollutant affecting Henry could take months and that this would be beyond our financial resources. In fact we were struggling financially all round. We had to fund all the care and equipment for the boys, and it was proving to be too much for us. No family members had offered financial help with the vast burden of caring for the boys. So John's generosity went straight to my heart.

He took samples of blood from me and from Henry and explained that he didn't think it would be necessary to take a sample from Michael in the first analysis. I knew it would be a while before John got back to me. He would have to test numerous substances in turn, and as this was a little like looking for a needle in a haystack it would take time.

Several months later John phoned me to say he had a result and would I come over to see him. I shot over there. John had a wonderful way of explaining things in very simple terms without being the slightest bit patronising. He explained that he had gone through every test available and had eventually found the same pattern in both Henry and me. He said it would appear that mercury was the culprit. He explained that an allergy to mercury suppresses the enzyme which allows the body to absorb magnesium. And magnesium is vital for brain function. He said he hoped that by injecting Henry intramuscularly with several high doses of magnesium he could bypass the guts, where the allergy was, and kick-start the enzyme into working.

I was so relieved that finally someone had given us an answer. I didn't feel any guilt about being in some way 'responsible', I had long since shed such feelings. The news that Henry's condition could be traced to mercury poisoning was shocking but it also opened up the possibility of treatment.

Two days later we started injecting Henry. He had six doses of magnesium in total, two a week for three weeks. The results were astounding. Henry's fits reduced overnight and his floppiness diminished so much that he was able to stand and walk, holding on to two people for balance.

John had sent our samples to the States to have the results verified with more sophisticated techniques. The same result came back – mercury poisoning. We privately rejoiced. Were we finally on the right track? Could this be the path to my vision – could Henry's problems be solved so simply? All the chit-chatting I did every day to my guides, guardian angels, God and anyone else who cared to listen seemed to be paying off at last.

Chapter 7

I used to have the boys' hair cut round the corner, at a little children's clothes shop set up by a delightful ex-City trader who had decided she'd had enough of stocks and shares and wanted to do something completely different. When we came in for a haircut a few weeks after Henry's magnesium treatment she immediately saw the difference in him. I told her the story and her jaw dropped. She told me she knew the features editor of *The Times* and that I should tell our story in public. I hesitated – this was a private matter and Henry was still right at the beginning of the treatment. Excited as I was, I wasn't sure we were ready to share it, but I told her to go ahead and see whether there was any interest.

I got home to find a message from the *Times* man waiting on our answering machine. Alarmed by how keen they were, I rang back and said I needed time to think about it. He quite understood and said he'd call back in a couple of weeks. He banged on about how it was of public interest and a story of hope. I said I'd let him know.

Two weeks later he called again. I don't know whether I was flattered or just feeble, but I agreed to do it. That very afternoon they sent round one of their top journalists, Mary Riddell. There was an instant rapport between us and I felt very relaxed with her. I spouted my story and Mary scribbled.

A few days later the feature appeared over more than half a page of *The Times*. It looked good, but we weren't sure what to expect next, if anything. The public response to the piece was astonishing. Over the next few days we were inundated with around two thousand calls and letters. The vast majority, about 98 per cent of them, were about boys under twelve, all displaying the same undiagnosed symptoms as Henry. Mary had also mentioned in the feature that I was setting up the Henry Spink Foundation, 'a charitable trust dedicated eventually to providing all that [I] lacked'. Many people sent in cheques. We sat there dumbfounded – this was like a dream come true. I could hardly believe that people were responding to what I had done with such respect and appreciation.

Michael's firm, Spink and Son, was next door to Christie's, the famous auction house in London's West End, and over the years we'd met dozens of people in the art world at various social functions. Suddenly we were getting calls from many of them, some saying they had never known that we had disabled children, others admitting that they too had a disabled child and had not been able to talk openly about it.

The feature turned out to be a godsend. It gave us the money to get the Foundation going and added weight to our credibility. If *The Times* was talking about the Foundation, then it must be OK. Most importantly, our situation was now 'out there'. We could talk openly about it and people felt free to engage with us. It freed us from the taboos and the sense of fear and shame surrounding disability. Before the article, even good friends had felt cagey about mentioning anything, in case they upset an already fragile situation. Now that our situation was public knowledge friends as well as strangers shed their reserve and approached us with warmth and interest.

As soon as the *Times* feature appeared I was telephoned by Viva Radio and asked to come and speak on a programme the same day.

'Well, I . . .' I mumbled, paralysed with terror at the prospect.

'Great,' they told me. 'A taxi's on its way.'

I'm not a natural spokesperson. I've shied away from any form of public speaking since I was five years old and I froze on the spot in the school nativity play, unable to deliver the one paltry line I'd practised so hard. Now here I was about to speak off-the-cuff to an audience of thousands. I was so numb with fear that I could hardly think straight.

I arrived at the Viva headquarters and was pushed straight into the recording studio where I was handed a pair of headphones and immediately bombarded with questions. I hadn't realised it was live, which was probably just as well. Amazingly, I found my voice and it went fine, although I left feeling I'd just been tossed in an emotional whirlwind and spat out. Still, I felt proud of myself and grinned all the way home. Later I learned that my family and Michael's had listened to the broadcast and they all told me how well it had gone.

I got home to find a message from *Woman's Hour* on

BBC Radio 4. Would I go on their programme too? I gulped. Doing it once with no time to think about it was one thing, but this was far more terrifying. Not only was *Woman's Hour* a hugely well-known and prestigious programme, but I'd have plenty of time to prepare – and to get even more panic-stricken. I knew I was being wimpish and that if I wanted to make the Foundation a success I had to get involved in public events. I thought about David telling me to find the courage to get off the fence. This qualified as a definite fence moment. I agreed to go on the programme, and immediately began to feel sick.

The broadcast was scheduled for three weeks' time, during which I developed a terrible cough and could hardly speak. I felt sure they would cancel it. The day before I was due on air one of their researchers called me to ask a few more questions. I had the most dreadful tickle in my throat and could hardly speak. After grilling me for about twenty minutes she finally commented on my continuous hacking and asked if I would be able to get through the broadcast.

'Oh,' I said. 'Yes, I'll be fine!'

The next day a taxi arrived for me. As I sat in the waiting room at the studio my heart was pounding so fast I was convinced I was about to have a heart attack. At least I'd be spared the ordeal of making a fool of myself. Minutes later I was ushered into an incredibly smart, plush room in which Jenni Murray, legendary presenter of *Woman's Hour*, sat waiting for me. I donned the headphones and Jenni launched in. I lowered my voice and spoke clearly and slowly. I felt as though it was someone far away who was talking, not me at all. Then it was over and they were all patting me on the back saying how incredibly well I'd done. They too were inundated with callers in a similar situation.

We did, however, have one very unpleasant experience as a result of the publicity. We were approached by a London-based Russian 'scientific group' who claimed that they had invented the most miraculous ways of detoxifying the system. All they needed was a urine sample, which they would analyse for free. Their claims sounded so real, and as vulnerable and naïve parents we longed for them to be true. We sent off Henry's sample.

Three weeks later we received a letter saying that they could cure Henry 100 per cent – but that their treatment would cost £12,000, or we could pay them £4,000 to keep Henry's condition stable. They added that if we didn't have their treatment our child would rapidly deteriorate. I wondered how many other desperate parents had been approached and how many had remortgaged their houses for the promises of this manipulative and immoral blackmailing scheme. It showed us how many people there are willing to make a quick buck out of others' distress, and gave me the incentive to write a checklist of questions for parents to ask before embarking on any treatment.

Now that the publicity had brought in some money and we were becoming known, it was time to get the Foundation up and running. We felt we needed to launch the charity with an event and were slightly at a loss about what to do and how to do it. Then we had a call from Lady Carolyn Townsend, an events organiser, who had

read the *Times* piece. She offered us one of her forthcoming events, a Halloween Ball, as a fund-raiser for the
Foundation. I immediately said yes, not knowing who
she was or anything about her organisation. In fact, as I
later discovered, her company organised many of the
most successful events on the London social scene.

Our event – known as the Black Cat Ball – was to be
held at the Natural History Museum. We set up a
committee – me, Michael, Maggie and a few friends –
to help Carolyn's team organise it. We had just eight
weeks in which to sort out tables, menus, caterers, a
band, raffles and prizes, goody bags for each guest,
decorations, flowers . . . Oh, and to sell five hundred
tickets, which we still had to design and print. Plenty of
time, I thought. If I'd known what it was going to
involve, panic might have paralysed me right at the
beginning – but luckily I was blissfully ignorant. Carolyn's team were fabulous and fitted in well with our
own. Our biggest challenge was selling the tickets: it
wasn't going to be easy to shift four hundred at £100
each for the sit-down dinner and another hundred more
modestly priced tickets for after-dinner guests.

All the teachers and helpers from Henry's school were
invited to come for free. I knew none of them were on
salaries that would stretch to luxury-priced tickets, but to
me they deserved every bit of thanks we could give. I
hoped that this small gesture would show them how
grateful we were for the care and love they give these
vulnerable children and their families. On the night of the
ball I think they enjoyed the whole thing more than any
other guests – it was a real pleasure to see.

By mid-October, with two weeks to go, everything was looking good, though we still had a fair number of tickets to sell. Getting it to this stage had been intensely hard work and hugely stressful, but great fun too. As the day approached we were beginning to get nervous about shifting the remaining tickets. We targeted companies, every kind we could think of from breweries to banks, along with people from the art world plus our families and friends. I also wrote to a number of celebrities, hoping they'd attract press coverage for us if they came. I'd learned, by this time, that the press was going to be a vital ally in making the Foundation a success.

I had also begun to learn the value of networking. There was always someone who could help with whatever task I had in hand – it was just a question of finding them. I discovered that if I asked ten people for help with a problem, at least one would oblige or know someone who could.

I wanted to make sure we had press coverage of the ball so I asked my aunt if she happened to know anyone I could ask. She did, and promptly put me in touch with John Rendell of *Hello!* magazine. John said he'd cover the event and wanted to tell our story too. This was far more than I'd expected – I'd have been grateful for just a picture of the ball with a caption. Our story was a long way from the celebrity-filled, glamorous style of *Hello!* and I wondered what angle they would take. They sent round a delightful writer, but Michael resolutely refused to have the photographer in our house. He had heard about the 'curse of *Hello!*' and how every happy couple pictured in their home by the magazine seemed to get divorced soon afterwards. My aunt Maggie saved the day by offering to have the shoot done in her house. Perhaps not the wisest move, since not long afterwards she divorced!

The day was a nightmare from beginning to end. The photographer wanted endless shots of us running round the garden, Michael carrying Freddie on his shoulders and me walking Henry. It didn't help that the ground was a minefield of thousands of dog turds deposited by my aunt's foul, ankle-biting Pekinese. Luckily the dog had been locked away for the day to avoid it savaging the photographer and landing us with a lawsuit. After two hours we took a break. At which point Freddie, who at almost five was able to shuffle along on his bottom, quietly sidled over to the case containing all the photographer's films and started to pull the used ones apart, exposing them to the light and rendering them useless. By chance one of the photographer's assitants spotted him and whisked him away just in time to save half of them! The day was hideously long and by the end even my aunt, who'd only had to observe, looked quite haggard.

When the feature appeared five days before the ball we were spread across three pages, with eight photographs. The headline read: 'Henrietta Spink tells of her eight-year battle for a better future for her sons: Mobilising her aristocratic, royal and showbusiness connections on behalf of all parents of disabled children.' I roared with laughter. They'd got their celebrity angle. And it was true, I was mobilising like mad. But as for my connections, I'd never even met my aristocratic relatives – we'd been firmly sidelined after my father left – still, it was true that they, like the showbiz people I'd made contact with, had responded to a persuasive letter or two. And the piece was great, everyone was delighted and *Hello!* agreed to give us a full page of coverage for the ball.

A week before the event I felt truly exhausted. Launching the charity was turning out to be a twenty-four-hour job, and that was on top of caring for the boys, running the house and trying to keep up with my bookbinding work. Something had to go. The obvious choice was to let the bookbinding go, but I was deeply reluctant as it was my only income. As Trustees of the Foundation Michael and I could not be paid. I could fundraise to pay other people's salaries, but I could not receive a cent myself. My small bookbinding salary had paid for extras like the odd holiday, clothes or decorating the house. Giving it up was a bitter pill to swallow, but I had no choice. The Foundation was so badly needed that I couldn't stop now. I knew we would manage somehow: God would provide and money would be forthcoming.

Tina Stallard, a close friend whose husband Hugh is godfather to Henry, was a producer for BBC News and she'd just been offered the opportunity to produce a mini-film on any theme she chose. She had been thinking about doing a film on 'a day in the life of a clamper'. Then suddenly Henry's face popped into her mind. Tina rang to ask if I would be willing to take part in her mini-film and to tell Henry's story. I cheerfully agreed, without any real idea of what it would involve. I rather naïvely thought that if it was a ten-minute film it might take a couple of hours to put together.

How wrong I was. The filming took place just days

before the ball and our house was invaded with film paraphernalia and a full film crew for three solid days. The good part was that I wasn't in the slightest bit nervous as I knew this was just a BBC exercise. I'm not sure I even got round to brushing my hair before I was interviewed. I was feeling so haggard from organising the ball that I'd given up bothering to look in the mirror.

When the film was finished Tina took it back to the BBC to edit. At which point Tina's boss took one look, loved the story and immediately edited it down to a news feature and put it on the 1 p.m., 6 p.m. and 9 p.m. main news. Fergus Walsh, the BBC's health correspondent, introduced the story, which was centred on the discovery of Henry's mercury allergy and his improvement since his injections. The date was 31 October, the night of our ball. I couldn't have wished for more perfect timing.

Getting ready for the ball was hilarious. That afternoon I'd had my hair done at Fortnum and Mason, who specialised in putting up long hair. When I'd got home Freddie had ignored me as I plainly wasn't Mummy any more, while Henry had grinned up at me and, at the speed of lightning, plunged both his hands into my hairdo. Trying to get his hands out without the whole thing collapsing took some skill. As did removing the spaghetti hoops a couple of hours later, after I'd shovelled dinner into the boys.

With an hour to go I got into the dress I'd bought at the last minute. I'm not a good shopper and had been reluctant to spend money. I'd debated for ages about whether just to borrow a dress, but in the end had splashed out on a gorgeous blue silk ballgown. It was very elegant, off the shoulder, with a tight-waisted bodice and full skirt. I had also asked whether Spink and Son would lend me a necklace. They'd been somewhat loath to, as only the week before a rather flamboyant member of staff had borrowed a pair of stunning and very valuable emerald earrings, got roaring drunk and lost one in the cab on the way home. Spink cautiously agreed to lend me one of their rather less resplendent necklaces. That was fine with me – less risky, and it looked lovely.

Sitting in the back of a cab with Michael on the way to the Natural History Museum, dressed in our finery, I was filled with delicious nerves. But I was determined to trust that the evening would be fine and to enjoy it. We'd worked so hard for it that I wasn't going to let nerves get in the way now.

The ball was to be held in the great entrance hall of the museum, which houses an enormous dinosaur. Dining and dancing would happen under and around the dinosaur. Row upon row of round tables were exquisitely adorned with lavish scented flowers and goody bags. Halloween decorations covered every spare inch of the place – it looked stunning. I couldn't believe this extravaganza was our event. Very soon the guests began to arrive, some in traditional ballgowns, others in full Halloween costume dripping with blood and gore. One after another they announced they had seen the *Six O'Clock News* and congratulated us. It felt very surreal; being centre stage was a whole new experience.

To produce a stunning meal for four hundred is quite a feat, but everything went incredibly smoothly. All sorts of side-shows had been laid on. There were palm readers, mediums, wishing trees with the most lavish prizes attached to them, raffles, tombolas and stalls. I decided to pop in and see one of the mediums. Everyone got a five- to ten-minute reading, so I sat down not expecting anything too serious. The medium looked at me and said that I'd be approached to write a book, become involved in politics and be a spokeswoman on education. She said I would become notorious in the health sector and that my children would be healed. I sat there dumbfounded. Politics and a spokesperson – yuk, I thought. I hated any form of public speaking. A book – ha! Even more unlikely – I couldn't spell to save my life. The only thing I knew she was right about was that my boys would be healed. I hadn't mentioned that I had children, so I felt very happy with this aspect of her prediction, but my mind was left whirring about the rest.

There was one extra event that evening that I shall truly cherish – it certainly made the launch of the Henry Spink Foundation even more memorable. Bob and Lindsey Hall were delightful friends of ours; they were also art dealers and were looking forward to the evening. They had put on elaborate fancy dress costumes and looked fantastic – we hardly recognised them.

Lindsey was nine months pregnant and her baby was due the next day. Since her previous children had all been late, she was damned if she was going to miss a good party. But the moment she sat down for dinner, her waters broke. Our phone call asking for an ambulance to come to the Natural History Museum in the middle of the evening was met with some scepticism the other end, particularly as there were raucous party noises going on in the background. Eventually they did pitch up and little Genevieve arrived in time for her birth to be announced during the after-dinner speeches. Great cheers of congratulation roared through the hall.

Carriages were at midnight, though no one wanted such a good party to end. I don't think Michael or I slept much that night, we were both on such a high. The next day Fergus Walsh rang Michael to say that our news feature had received the largest response to any BBC feature in his entire time there. We were about to be inundated, once again, with calls and letters from the public.

Chapter 8

Towards the end of 1995 Angela, our lovely nanny, had left us. After almost four years I dreaded being without her companionship and support. We had grown as close as sisters, but I knew it was time for her to do something different. She was exceptionally bright and had studied English to a very high standard. Now she wanted to train to be a lawyer and we were delighted for her, though it didn't stop us both sobbing for weeks before she left.

We had advertised again in the Aussie paper, the *TNT*, and this time it produced Jodie. She was brassy, brash and very bold. After Angela's gentleness, Jodie's gung-ho style scared the hell out of me, particularly around Freddie. She would pick him up and spin him in circles before chucking him on to the sofa. When I first saw her do this I was really alarmed. We still thought of Freddie as very fragile; he'd had one bug or another almost constantly since he was born, on top of the major surgery he'd endured as a baby. But Freddie loved Jodie's games and squealed with laughter as he landed on the sofa. We began to realise that he wasn't as fragile as we'd thought. Though he was still small and rather weedy, he didn't need to be treated like cut glass. Jodie's view of him, as a little boy who loved to play, was fresh and new and taught us to reassess the way we treated him.

Jodie was a true Aussie. In London there is a delightful little place where the Aussies congregate, called the Church. Not a pew or an altar in sight, though – this Church is a large barn. The floor is covered with saw-dust, to absorb all the puke from the serious drinking bouts which go on through the day and into the night. Most of the congregation have passed out by the end of the day. Jodie would regularly traipse in at two in the morning after a session in the Church, waking the kids up and crashing out on her floor if she didn't quite make the bed. Complaints the next morning rarely resulted in anything more than a very sullenly hungover 'Sorry'.

Jodie adored both boys and they her. She drove me nuts at times, but we got on well and she always made me laugh. She taught me how to take a lot less nonsense from people. Her approach was totally blunt and to the point – if you don't like it, say so. On one very funny occasion in Covent Garden a pushy gypsy approached Jodie and handed her a small bunch of lucky heather. Jodie took it, said 'Thank you' and walked on. At which point the gypsy shouted after her that she wanted a pound for it. Without slowing her pace or glancing back, Jodie flung the offending sprig over her shoulder with a gruff '**** off.' It took me half an hour to stop laughing.

At this time Michael and I were virtually always broke. Caring for one disabled child costs the equivalent of caring for three regular children. So our income, now without my contribution, was being stretched to care for the equivalent of six children. It was a tough call.

Michael had organised a successful art exhibition at Spink and Son the previous summer, and during the spring of 1996 had received a small bonus as a result of the good turnover the exhibition generated. We decided to blow it on a two-week holiday in Cornwall. The country's stunning landscapes would be a wonderful contrast to the open flatness of Norfolk where we normally spent our holidays.

We rented a beautiful Georgian house owned by a lovely couple called Juliet and Anthony, with whom we instantly became great friends. The house was on the Lizard Peninsula, close to the Helford River, one of the most beautiful rivers in England. Michael and his family had spent many childhood summers on the Helford River. His family were nearly all keen sailors and knew the territory well. He and his brothers, sister and father would sail the family's small yacht while his mother, who easily became sea-sick and preferred to stay on dry land, supplied the troops with vast quantities of sandwiches. Michael hadn't been back to Cornwall for years and we were in dire need of a break, so we both looked forward to it with real excitement.

When the day arrived the car was packed to the gunwales with all the paraphernalia we needed for the boys. Wheelchairs, special loo seats, side-protectors for Henry's bed, special drinking mugs – you name it, we'd packed it. The boot and roof rack were literally bursting at the seams and our car must have looked like something out of a circus.

The drive was long and whenever Jodie, who was seated between the boys in the back of the car, nodded off, Freddie amused himself by winding down the window and quietly hurling things out, including his shoes.

We eventually had to stop the car, dismantle the door and remove the handle to stop him opening the window. His other favourite trick was to undo his seat belt, lean forward and suddenly grab the gear stick and whip it out of gear. Freddie had developed an amazing ability to observe mechanical things and understand how they functioned, and he understood exactly how the car was driven.

Car journeys with the boys were never easy, but the worst was a journey I had taken back from Surrey after visiting a friend. We'd set off on a dual carriageway with no hard shoulder where I could stop. It had begun to pour with rain and, as lightning and thunder clattered overhead, driving conditions were becoming worse by the minute. Suddenly Henry started to fit and began to slide under his seat belt, which trapped him by his neck. Freddie, who had eaten supper just before we left, was now beginning to regurgitate his food. The pressure from his seat belt had obviously given his stomach a spasm and vomit was now coming out of his nose. As I glanced back at one child turning a mottled blue and the other streaming with vomit I wondered whether, by the time I found a suitable stopping place, my children would still be alive.

The result of this nightmare journey was that I hated travelling on my own with the boys. But even with Michael and Jodie along too it was no picnic. We'd fill the pockets in the backs of the front seats with toys for both boys to play with. This was fine until Freddie suddenly decided to hurl them at us in the front seats. Later on, when he was able to say a few words, he'd simultaneously say 'Sorr. . . . ee' as he threw each offending object. We couldn't help but laugh – it was impossible to keep a straight face.

Henry was angelic in the car. He was totally happy to feel the sensation of the car in motion and listen to classical music. Unfortunately Freddie hated it – he wanted Disney or his other sugary favourites, but these only made Henry howl. The answer, once they were old enough, was separate cassette players, with headphones, for each of them. Freddie had an amazing memory, particularly for music. He'd remember every track on a tape and the exact order in which they'd been played. He also knew the moment that the last song ended and would announce it by furiously pointing at the stereo or cassette player to indicate to us that it needed turning over.

Nerves barely intact, we eventually arrived in Cornwall. Our holiday house was up a grand gated driveway and looked wonderful. Juliet and Anthony greeted us and warmly welcomed the boys. We unloaded the car while our hosts looked on in polite disbelief at the sheer volume of equipment we'd brought. Inside, the house felt terribly grand. Most of the rooms would comfortably have accommodated the whole of our London house. It was beautiful and within a few hours we'd settled in.

That night Michael and I decided to go for supper at the Shipwright's Arms, a delightful pub in Helford village, overlooking the river. The views were spectacular and we sat gazing out over the sea as delicious smells from the barbecue wafted our way. We ordered food and sipped our wine, and at that moment everything seemed so perfect that I wished time could stand still. I wanted to make the evening last for ever. It was, for a brief moment, as if all the stresses and strains of caring for the boys had vanished.

I still believed in my vision of Henry healed and well. In fact the vision had become clearer as the years had passed. I almost felt I could walk into the library where Henry was reading, and sit watching him. I'd never been able to 'tune in' to Freddie in quite the same way, but none the less I felt he too would emerge from his disability. I knew that to most people what I felt was irrational, foolish or misguided. But to me it made perfect sense and, though I got frustrated as time went by, my longing to see my boys healed and my belief that it would happen never diminished.

Michael and I often discussed my vision for the boys. He was totally supportive; not once did he ever suggest that I might be fantasising, or criticise me. He said he loved what I saw, he just wished he could see it too. It wasn't that he didn't believe me – he just couldn't feel convinced in the way I did.

That evening, as we sat beside the river, I started to talk of other pictures or scenarios that I had seen in my mind. There were times, particularly when I was restoring a manuscript, when I became almost meditational and all kinds of images would float into my mind. One of them was a vision of winning money, which I'd often mentioned to Michael.

The sun was beginning to set and had turned the sea a golden pink. The water was as calm as a pond and the gentle lapping of the waves against the boats moored alongside us added to the already hypnotic atmosphere.

We wandered slowly back along the lane, past the enchanting thatched cottages, to the end of the creek where you could cross over a small wooden bridge and contemplate the view or continue round on the road. We ambled on to the bridge and stood in the middle, staring out to sea.

I hated to break the peaceful silence, but felt an overwhelming need to speak. I have no idea what prompted me to say what I did next, but the timing, for once in my life, seemed right.

I said, 'If we win some money – and I mean substantial money – in the next few weeks, will you believe me about Henry and Freddie?'

Michael, slightly taken aback, turned and looked at me. 'Sure thing,' he said.

We mulled over the idea of what we would do when we won the money. Michael suggested we buy a house in Cornwall. I liked the idea. I was tired of Norfolk and the endless problems we had renting my aunt's house. We'd turn up at midnight to find the place freezing and dirty. Arriving on holiday exhausted and with two fragile children in tow, only to have to make beds, clean the house and then pay a substantial rent, didn't feel like much of a break. So the idea of our own retreat in this idyllic setting seemed like a wonderful idea. I agreed, and as far as I was concerned the deal was done and we would be purchasing a house.

The holiday was relaxing and fun, despite the hard work that caring for the boys always entailed. There was still the endless laundry, and the food preparation took a large chunk of each day. Henry hated to chew and he was really fussy about textures. Fish fingers or burgers were definitely not his idea of a meal. We had to cook fresh food and he expected a varied menu – no meal could be served twice in the same week or he'd howl with outrage and refuse to eat it. Freddie, now four and a half, wasn't quite so fussy but he had problems swallowing. Increasingly often he would choke on a mouthful of food which would then take a couple of hours to clear. We had no idea what was going on and related it to behavioural problems as he always seemed so angry. This pattern of choking was beginning to happen at every meal, and we prayed it would disappear.

We returned to London feeling well rested. The only cloud on the horizon was that Jodie's visa was running out and she had decided to return to Australia. This meant we had to start advertising immediately for someone to replace her, as I couldn't manage the boys without help. Within a couple of weeks of the ad appearing, a nice young Australian arrived. She told us she had loads of experience with special needs kids and was open and friendly. We asked for her references and rang a couple in Australia. All seemed well and we decided to take her on. But it wasn't long before we hit problems. Her room turned into a squalid tip, as did the bathroom. I asked her politely to clean her room and got a furious outburst about why she shouldn't have to do such things and how she should be free to behave any which way she chose. At the time I had a lot on my plate, with the Foundation work on top of caring for the boys. I also had no idea how to handle her lack of hygiene and her tantrums. So, despite my qualms, I just ignored the situation and told myself I'd deal with it later.

That autumn a client of Michael's, a lovely man called Douglas, invited Michael out to Thailand and Cambodia on a business trip. Spink and Son agreed to pay for him to go. I was to be left behind as usual – I felt miserable. And then, I have no idea why, out of the blue Douglas offered to pay for me to go too. I couldn't believe it: this would be our first chance to be alone together since our honeymoon. It would also, of course, be the first time I'd ever left the boys. The week before we left I went downstairs to get the mail. As I bent down to pick it up I noticed a form for the football pools. I had always assumed I'd win my money on the lottery – I played a pound a week and that was all I did. But on that day something made me fill in the pools form. It had ten numbers as opposed to the six numbers for the lottery. This suited me far better! I had a host of lucky numbers, including all our birth numbers and the charity's number.

A year or so earlier I'd been so sure of my win that I'd penned a rather illiterate note about winning the lottery and the boys being healed. I decided to seal it in an envelope and leave it with a local solicitor. I saw it as an affirmation and also as proof that I'd seen it before it happened. I explained to the solicitor, who probably thought I was quite dotty, that this was a prediction. I asked him to sign it on the back, across the seal of the envelope, with the date, and to keep it safe for me. Then I posted off the pools form and forgot all about it in the chaos of preparing for our trip.

We were to be away for ten days and organising the boys' care was a nightmare. To our delight our old nanny, Angela, offered to come and look after them with our not quite perfect present nanny. She refused to be paid, telling us she was missing the boys horribly and was thrilled to have an opportunity to spend time with them. Her generosity to us and to the boys remained constant, and we felt we could never thank her enough. I had to prepare and freeze all the boys' meals in advance. Feeling as though I was organising a military campaign, I sweated for over a week to get it all done. Much as I looked forward to the trip, I was also filled with trepidation at the idea of leaving the boys.

When the day came for us to leave I felt numb. It was a real wrench, but I knew it was important for Michael and me to spend some time together. We'd had eight years with the boys, with barely a break. It was time to let go a little. Besides, travelling and exploring had always been a dream of mine, one which I'd had to put aside since the boys arrived. Now was my chance to see somewhere completely new, and I was going to enjoy every minute of it.

When we arrived in Bangkok we were met by Douglas's chauffeur and ushered through customs. Douglas had lent us one of his apartments, which was truly luxurious; I felt as if I'd died and gone to heaven. He'd even laid on a personal chef who would cook anything we wanted. The next day we headed for Phnom Penh, where we stayed in a rather shabby hotel and that night ate under the stars in a restaurant perched high up a steep hillside. Douglas's chauffeur downed an entire bottle of whisky and still drove us back to the hotel afterwards, much to my amazement.

The next morning we caught a small plane up to

Angkor. The hotel there was far shabbier than the last one and the restaurant a joke. The menu was rather sophisticated and was written in French, a leftover from colonial days, but it was in fact utterly redundant as all the chefs had been murdered by the former Khmer Rouge regime. Only unqualified youngsters remained, so the food that was on offer was very basic. However, Douglas insisted on choosing Crêpe Suzette from the menu just to see what they'd do. The waiters disappeared to discuss what Crêpe Suzette might actually be. After much discussion they eventually came back with something which looked rather like scrambled eggs with syrupy goo poured over the top. With a twinkle in his eye Douglas told the waiter serving this sticky mess that it was not Crêpe Suzette at all and he should go and get the chef to explain himself. A few minutes later the waiter returned to say, 'Chef not coming.'

'Why not?' Douglas asked.

To which the waiter replied that the chef, too frightened to make his appearance, had departed via the back window and gone home.

There are not enough words to describe the beauty of the lost city of Angkor. It is awesome, majestic and, at times, terrifying. It covers a larger area than the whole of London, and the sheer power and volume of its magnificence were truly overwhelming. Many of the temples and buildings had been swallowed by the jungle and we'd travel great distances to find stunning remains almost consumed by giant trees. Whole boulders would be lifted up and sucked into the roots of trees – it was something out of *The Day of the Triffids*.

Lining every walkway to every temple were rows of heartbreakingly damaged children. All were missing limbs, blown off by the endless landmines laid by the Khmer Rouge. Some children had lost all four limbs and their eyes. The pitiful sight of these part-human forms with their little begging bowls and pleading faces was too much to bear. These were the lost children of the lost city.

Few tourists were visiting at the time and they travelled in tour groups, as the danger of landmines and kidnap by the Khmer Rouge was still very real. When we wanted to visit a particularly beautiful temple off the beaten track, called Banteay Srei, we had to arrange for armed guards to take us. Only a week before, two Australians had been shot while visiting the temple. Douglas made us rather nervous by telling us he suspected it was the guards who'd shot the tourists. It certainly gave them plenty of lucrative work. Perhaps they felt that the odd tourist could be sacrificed to promote business!

The guards rode on motorcycles ahead of us with their automatic rifles slung over their shoulders. Douglas took the slightly unusual precaution of filming them through-out the trip as evidence, in case they turned their guns on us. The trip went off without a hitch, but there was a moment when all of us froze in terror at the distant sound of what we thought was gunfire. The guards laughed and said it was a car going over a rickety wooden bridge.

Our stay passed all too quickly. I did miss the boys horribly, but in truth it was great to be away from the endless cycle of drudgery and caring that totally domi-nated my life. I felt as if I was on temporary release from prison and wondered when my next break would be. The night before we were due to fly home Michael and I were relaxing in our hotel room before heading out to supper. The trip had been exhilarating but tiring, and I was lying on the bed while Michael was reading a book. The phone rang and it was Angela in London. She spoke to Michael, who went grey and then white and sat down. He stared blankly at me as if he couldn't take in what Angela was saying.

Someone from the football pools had come round to our house. I smiled – I knew my boys would be well.

Chapter 9

We decided to keep the news of our windfall to ourselves. In the past we had seen various programmes on television about people who had won money and whose lives had been ruined by the uninvited opinions and greed of those around them. I had jokingly mentioned to my family, some time before, that I had foreseen a financial windfall. Their reaction had been to look green with envy and then start telling us what we should and should not do with it. At the time I found it a little bizarre that they seemed to believe me, especially when they were so cynical about my vision for the boys. That evening in Cornwall, when Michael and I had discussed what we would do if my premonition of winning money came true, we had agreed we wouldn't tell anybody. Why invite problems? So when, a year later, Angela called us in Thailand she knew to keep it a secret too.

Our last day in Bangkok was quite surreal. We had no idea how much we'd won. We knew it had to be a reasonable amount because the pools representative had visited in person; but it could have been a sum like £25,000, which would be lovely but wouldn't radically alter our lives. Savouring the 'not knowing' was in itself delicious. Deep inside I was revelling in the sure knowledge that if I'd been right on this I was sure as hell going to be right about the boys becoming well. Both visions had been equally clear. Michael and I couldn't stop smiling. Winning money, having foreseen it, would be classed as exotic and wonderful, but finding a cure for Henry would be classed as miraculous. Yet I knew now, categorically, that we would eventually find the answer for the boys, and I felt honoured to have been chosen for the task of finding it.

The moment our plane touched down in London I was desperate to see my boys – it was as if I'd neatly shelved my maternal emotions while I was away, and now suddenly they were back in full force. I wanted to run home and thought I'd expire with frustration as the taxi crawled along through the morning traffic. Eventually we got there and raced inside to gather both boys on to our laps for hugs. I couldn't believe how much they seemed to have grown. They were thrilled to see us and had clearly had a great time while we were away. Angela was a real surrogate mother to them and I knew she had cared for them brilliantly. As we handed out our gifts I could see her trying to catch my eye, desperate for me to call the pools people. In fact she was far more eager than I was to know the outcome. I guess I was still savouring the fact that we'd won, which I felt so certain meant that the rest of my prediction would follow. I was glowing with joy and acceptance. Angela eventually dragged me to the phone. I hesitated, suddenly full of trepidation. Would it be enough money just to pay off our debts and have a good holiday, or would it make a real difference to us? I slowly dialled the number, my heart hammering.

A man with a strong Yorkshire accent answered the phone.

I began, 'Hi, it's Mrs Spink. You came round to our house while we were away.'

He replied cheerfully, 'Hello. Did you know you've won some money?'

I said, 'Yes.' By this time I felt so nervous I was chewing my nails.

'How do ye fancy fifty grand?' he said.

'Yes, please,' I replied.

'How do ye fancy a hundred grand?'

'That would be lovely,' I said.

'Well, how do ye fancy a hundred and fifty grand?'

'Even better,' I said.

This went on for a while. Michael, who was watching me, looked so frustrated I thought he'd self-implode before our friend on the end of the line got to the final figure. My heart was racing faster and faster. Finally the Yorkshireman, who was loving every minute of our suspense, reached the princely sum of £350,200.09.

A silence followed while I tried to digest the information he'd just given me. I felt truly speechless. What do you say to a stranger who has imparted such extraordinary life-changing news? 'Thank you' seemed a little paltry in the circumstances, but I couldn't think of anything else to say.

He asked, 'Is it right that you've never played before?'

I said, 'Yes, and I shall probably never play again!' I didn't know whether to laugh or cry. Relief, gratitude, disbelief and exultation began to well up within me all at once. I asked Michael to take the phone – just to be sure I had not misheard the amount and written it down incorrectly. He scribbled down the amount – and no, I hadn't been wrong!

Michael, who was looking white as a sheet, asked him what we should do next. The Yorkshireman gave us the address of a hotel in South Kensington where the cheque would be handed over to us whenever we wanted to collect it. We said we'd be right over – it was only a ten-minute drive from our house.

After he'd put the phone down Michael and I sat and looked at each other and just beamed – neither of us could think of anything to say. It was one of those moments that you wish would last for ever. Most people have no warning that something this wonderful will happen. But, convinced it was coming, we'd had over a year to think about it. So we knew exactly what we were going to do with it. Our dream of a cottage in Cornwall was about to come true.

We got into the car and drove over to what turned out to be a small, nondescript hotel. We'd decided to leave the boys at home, which was a wrench having only just returned, but we both felt this was something we wanted to savour on our own. At the reception desk we asked if there was a representative from the pools company there to meet us. Everyone grinned. They suggested we take a seat over by the window. Did we want coffee? We said no – our stomachs were churning far too much with excitement. We sat and waited, holding hands.

Eventually a rather formal man in a suit appeared. He smiled, shook our hands and congratulated us warmly. He said there were a few formalities and a form to sign and asked us if we wanted publicity. We said no, none at all, thank you. That was fine – no problem. We signed the form and were handed the cheque. It seemed unreal to think that I had sat in my office only a few weeks earlier, pondering over which of our lucky numbers to use on the pools entry. I could hardly comprehend the result. Here I was, holding a piece of paper that would now truly transform our lives for the better.

Grinning like a couple of Cheshire cats, we decided to drive straight over to the bank and deposit the cheque. When we arrived and told them how much we wanted to deposit, the manager came out and ushered us into a side room. He was trying not to smile, but every now and then he'd catch our gaze and we could see the look of pleasure on his face. He knew our boys were disabled.

Having banked the cheque we drove home as fast as possible. The day passed in a blur, and I don't think we stopped buzzing for a single moment. The atmosphere was electric and the boys revelled in our new-found energy – it was completely infectious. There was something so delicious about knowing that no one else knew, bar Angela, who was happy to keep our secret. Neither of us even thought of going off and buying anything extravagant. Somehow we didn't need to – just knowing we'd won and dreaming about the cottage we were going to buy was enough. I don't think we even opened a bottle of champagne.

We discovered that our nanny had been rather a nightmare to Angela while we'd been away and, looking at her now, I felt worried. She clearly wasn't happy, and our obvious joy seemed to send her into further decline.

She was becoming openly hostile. When we mentioned to her that we'd won a small sum of money and were celebrating, she furiously replied that if we'd won something then she was now sure never to win anything. She reckoned that no two people in the same room could be that lucky. Her behaviour was becoming bizarre.

Later in the day I went up to my office, which was just below her room. As I reached the landing the stench that wafted down the stairs made me gag – it smelled as if an animal had died and was rotting. Holding my breath, I went up the stairs and into her room. The sight that greeted me was unbelievable. The floor was awash with dirty plates, cups furred with mould and bits of stale food. Piles of stinking unwashed clothing cascaded over every available surface. I couldn't face a confrontation and the row that would follow – not after ten days away and the amazing news we'd just had. I returned downstairs with a fixed smile on my face and didn't say a word. I decided I would deal with it later in the week.

In the event I didn't have to. We woke the next morning to find that she had gone. It was obviously all too much for her and she'd done a runner during the night. I was left with no help – not even Michael, as he had to go back to work – but for once I didn't care. I was on a high that nothing could destroy. And in truth her departure had saved us a lot of hassle – we'd have had to fire her anyway.

Before seeking a replacement I had to face the hideous job of cleaning her room. It was all I could do not to retch as I scraped the rotten food and used tampons off the floor. I wondered what on earth could be wrong with her. It was only later that we discovered she was a paranoid schizophrenic and on a cocktail of powerful drugs. Perhaps we'd got off lightly.

That done, I decided to call a few friends to see if they had any ideas for a new nanny. This time I wanted to get someone who came with a recommendation, rather than advertise or pay a fortune through an agency only to take my chances with whoever turned up. I rang Alex, a good chum, and she suggested I call a girl she had employed in the past who she believed was now between jobs. The girl's name was Janet. I suddenly remembered that the medium I had seen at the Halloween Ball a few weeks earlier had said that we would have a change of nanny and that a wonderful girl whose name would begin with J would come to us through a friend. Could this be her?

The moment I spoke to Janet I knew she was right for us. We clicked instantly, and we both knew we would get on brilliantly. I felt a surge of relief. Even with my new-found exuberance I knew it wasn't physically possible for me to manage the exhausting work of looking after the boys alone for long. Janet, who was twenty-four and came from Inverness in Scotland, came to see us the next day and was an instant hit. I hadn't felt this comfortable with anyone since Angela, and she immediately struck up a rapport with the boys. Michael and I sighed with thankfulness – it was wonderful to know we'd found someone so right. The only hitch was that Janet couldn't start until January – six weeks away. We'd have to survive on our own for that time. It would be tough, but we'd manage.

Michael and I were still fired up with excitement about

our win and the boys remained thrilled by our visible happiness. It saddened me to think that for much of the time they must have seen strain and anxiety on our faces. Of course we'd done our best to be cheerful. But life was so often a struggle, practically and emotionally, that however hard we tried it must have shown to the boys, both of whom were deeply sensitive. It was good to know that, for a while at least, they were seeing us relaxed and happy.

We decided to begin looking for our cottage as soon as possible, searched the Internet for somewhere to rent and found a little village house in the area we liked. We decided to take it for the week after Christmas. From there we could search for our dream house.

The weeks before Christmas were hard work but fun. I love this time of year and adore decorating absolutely everything in sight, including the tallest tree we can cram into the house. This had led to the odd mishap over the years. One Christmas, when the boys were tiny and we were still in our little two-up, two-down house, I staggered home, lifted my monster tree upright in and stuck it straight through the ceiling. In desperation I rang my sister, Cara, who knew all about specialised plastering techniques, and begged her to tell me what to do. After she'd finished laughing she gave me instructions and I got busy, guiltily blending a splash of black paint in with the white plaster to match the current grubby off-white colour of the ceiling. By the time Michael returned home that evening the tree was stunningly decorated and the repair so good that the join could barely be seen. But later that year the ceiling started to bulge rather alarmingly.

Michael gave it a prod with the end of the broom handle and the entire thing fell down. I'd clearly had a lucky escape with my tree!

Buoyed up as we were by the joy of our pools win, Christmas 1996 was fantastic. Everything sparkled and both boys adored it. For once I didn't have to worry about how much I spent on presents – it was such a great feeling.

Then we drove to Cornwall. The house we had rented was fairly shabby, but we didn't care; we were on a mission, and nothing was going to detract from that. The first morning we got up to find that a thin layer of snow had fallen during the night – incredibly rare for Cornwall, with its warmer climate than the rest of the country. We set off for the nearby town to trawl the estate agents, and arranged to view two properties straightaway. I wanted both boys to feel that they were 100 per cent part of this adventure. After all, the money had been a gift to all of us. Freddie, at five, was still small enough to be carried as we looked round. But Henry, who was about to turn nine, was just beginning to be too heavy for us, so, rather guiltily, we left him sitting in his buggy downstairs.

Neither of these first two cottages was for us, so we decided to go exploring to see if we could spot anything ourselves. It was a breathtakingly beautiful day. The sun was shining very brightly, frost sparkled everywhere and the snow still remained in the shadowy corners of fields. That day we drove all round the Lizard Peninsula. Towards the late afternoon we drove through a village on the edge of the Helford River, passing the village shop and a row of eighteenth- and nineteenth-century cottages. At the end of the row we spotted a very long, candy-pink, thatched cottage with a 'For Sale' sign outside it. In front of the cottage was the tiny village green, in the middle of which stood an ancient stone pillar inscribed with the name of a Celtic king.

We parked the car, and Michael rang the agent to ask whether we could view the property. The agent, keen not to miss a potential sale, raced over to meet us. The cottage had been on the market for over two years and the reason soon became apparent. The thatched roof was leaking badly and the cost of replacing it was immense; no one had wanted to take on the task. It had originally been built as three tiny workers' cottages a couple of hundred years earlier, and had at some stage been knocked through into one long building. It had a narrow staircase at either end and was one room deep, with four small bedrooms upstairs and a living room, kitchen and dining room downstairs. It had very low ceilings, but thankfully neither of us is very tall. No six-footers would have contemplated this house!

After a few minutes of wandering around, Michael and I looked at each other. We both knew this was perfect for us. We made an offer that day. As it was a cash offer with no chain involved we wanted to exchange in double-quick time, but this seriously annoyed the owner. Perhaps our enthusiasm led to doubts in his mind about whether he really wanted to sell the cottage. We could see his hesitation, but we pressed hard and after a bit of huffing and puffing he agreed.

We returned to London a week later, thrilled at the

prospect of our own rural bolt-hole. We knew it would change our lives and make the constant struggle so much more bearable. With the cottage to retreat to we'd survive. We exchanged contracts on Valentine's Day. We decided to tell family members that we'd won £50,000 and were going to use the money to rent the cottage in Cornwall. It explained the cottage, while giving us room to enjoy our win in private.

Winning the money gave us both fresh confidence. Not only did we have the enormous pleasure of our new hideaway, but it gave back some sorely needed faith. For the first time in a long while we believed that we were cared for and not just continually being singled out for a rough time. It was great to have a bit of respite from the toughness of life. We knew now that good things could – and did – happen to us.

Both of us felt less stressed and more relaxed than we had been for a long time. Michael continued with his job at Spink and Son and, with less pressure to earn money, was able to enjoy it more than he had in ages. Caring for our boys had been incredibly difficult, both practically and psychologically, for such a long time. The win seemed to give us a little respite, a chance to feel human again, to laugh and to believe in good things. The unrelieved slog went on, the same as ever. But it seemed a little easier because we felt happier. We felt full of optimism and hope.

Chapter 10

Janet arrived as planned in mid-January and I felt I'd found a true friend. She settled easily into the household and the boys loved her from the start. We were waiting to complete the purchase of the cottage, and over the next few weeks she and I had great fun drawing up lists of everything we'd need to kit it out from top to bottom. It was a bit like writing a wedding list with no limitations and no concessions to anyone else's taste. We had great fun.

Having some of the awful financial pressures lifted made our lives so much easier. As well as buying the cottage we were able to pay off half our mortgage and put aside money to help pay for the boys' future needs. But day-to-day life with them was still an uphill struggle much of the time. It was hard for anyone, even those close to us, to comprehend what it was like. Parents of normal children have so much to look forward to and celebrate. The first smile, sleeping through the night, first steps, first words, the end of nappies and all the milestones to follow.

We had none of this. Our boys had never walked or spoken – we'd never heard the words 'Mummy' or 'Daddy'. Both boys were still incontinent and needed nappies, and neither of them had ever slept through the night. We still had to get up for Henry three or four times a night, as he got his limbs tangled up and would shriek so loudly we were convinced half the road could hear him. And Freddie spent half of most nights awake. He would spread poo over his bed and anywhere else he could reach, then bottom-shuffle around coughing or vomiting because of the acid in his throat. Nothing seemed to help him. We tried raising his bedhead on bricks and we tried antacids, but neither made any difference. We both felt desperately worried about Freddie, but had no idea who to turn to.

The sleepless nights wore me out, and I often felt ill the next day when we'd been up five or six times during the night. Sometimes I despaired of our ever being able to sleep a whole night through. Michael seemed to cope better than me: he got up more often, and still managed to work the next day. Much of my day was taken up with cooking specialised food for the boys and with the endless cycles of laundry. It was a monotonous and never-ending routine.

Normal children have friends, and visit or go to parties. They get picked up and dropped off by friends and family. They stay with grandparents while the parents have a break. But there were no such arrangements for our family. Disabled children don't get asked to parties or go to people's houses. Friends can't just pick them up or have them for the afternoon. No one had ever offered to have the boys for us, even for one night. We understood why, but it was still very hard to take.

Life often felt very bleak. Caring for the boys was so relentless, and progress so slow. This continual grind with very little return was unbelievably sapping to one's spirit. Perhaps if we'd had one normal child things might have been different. We might have found a link to the world of normal children and families. But we had no foot in that camp, so we remained isolated. In a way we were so needy that people took one look at us and made every excuse under the sun not to get involved. I guess they thought that if they got sucked in it would never end. In some ways I felt I couldn't win. If I put on a brave face, everyone thought, 'Oh, good. She's coping, so we don't need to help', and if I went round weeping and saying I couldn't cope everyone ran a mile. None of it changed when we won the money, but somehow it all became more bearable. It was as if I could raise my head above the surface of the water and breathe fresh air before being submerged again.

Meanwhile I was spending every spare minute I had working for the Foundation. I'd been desperately anxious about stopping my bookbinding work and giving up my income. Now suddenly a lot of the worry was lifted, and I was able to throw myself into fundraising and getting the Foundation going. I had employed a girl called Sara, an ex-Spink and Son employee, to work as a researcher for the Foundation, and at the same time a London-based charity called Contact a Family approached me after reading about the Foundation in the press. They offered us an office within their premises.

I felt terrified – I was convinced they thought we were already an established charity and far further down the line than we actually were. Although we had raised some money and I had just employed my first researcher I still had no clear picture of exactly what we would do. It's one thing having an idea, but it's another thing translating it into reality.

I knew that if I was going to make this Foundation work I'd better get moving. I had no excuse. We had money and a Patron, the press was being supportive and now we were being offered premises. All wonderful gifts. So one afternoon I gathered a group of friends together and asked questions. What exactly, as parents of disabled kids, did we want? Bit by bit we hammered out some answers. We wanted unbiased, straightforward information on what alternative and conventional therapies were available. One of the issues that surfaced as we talked was our complete vulnerability. We were all on a mission to help our children to reach their potential or, God willing, to find a cure; and because of this we were very open to any possibilities, real or not, scrupulous or unscrupulous, which came our way.

Most of us had found that the conventional medical world was remarkably limited in what it could offer and extremely dispiriting in its attitude. As a result we turned to the fast-growing world of alternative therapies. Some of the therapies we found were extremely beneficial, but others were a complete con. It was often only after parents had invested serious amounts of money in something that was plainly never going to work that they started to ask the kind of questions they needed to have asked right at the beginning. We devised a checklist of questions that parents should ask before they embarked on any apparently miraculous therapy. We also designed a user-friendly format for the fact-sheets which would give parents information. We had a long way to go, but it was a start. Further help was about to come from a slightly unexpected quarter.

David, my lovely psychic healer, was moving away from London. I was going to miss his advice and support, but before he left he introduced me to a good friend of his, another medium called Peter.

I had reservations about going to see Peter because I was still smarting from the constant criticism from my mother that such encounters were evil. I felt rather cross with such criticism as only a year earlier she had sent Tilly off to David for some inspiration. However, I still felt desperate for insight into how to help my boys. It was all very well having a vision of the boys healed, but I needed to find a way to get there and any clues and insights that might help me were valuable. I decided that from now on I would not discuss with my mother any of my visits to mediums or what I learned from them. Having to make this decision saddened me because I'd like to have been able to talk to her about it, but it wasn't worth the arguments; I wanted a peaceful family life. When I went to see Peter I found he wasn't at all what I'd been expecting. Unlike David, who chatted away before we began the session, Peter was very professional and launched straight in with no small talk at all. He had a strong Irish accent and spoke incredibly fast, barely drawing breath. He gave me reams of information and it was hard to take on board everything he said. Thank God I was taping it.

The hour I spent with him was one of the most extraordinary of my life. It was as if he was laying before me my past, present and future in one fell swoop. What he said gave my life and the boys' births a reason and meaning in a way that nothing else had. Until then I'd felt as though my life was disjointed and the events in it completely random. Peter joined up the pieces and gave it continuity. He described life as being like a tidal sea that ebbs and flows with total harmony. He made me feel privileged to be on this journey and told me that I was being given no more than I was capable of dealing with and that I would definitely succeed.

The same themes I had heard before came up: the book, politics, campaigning and the healing of my children. But unlike previous mediums Peter gave me more detail. He talked of an American link, and said Americans would be behind the recovery of our children. He also indicated that we would live in the States part-time. I had no links with America and wondered how on earth this would come about. Peter described the Foundation going from strength to strength and said it would become known worldwide, and that I would become an educational campaigner. The information he gave me was very clear, but it was like pieces of a jigsaw that I still had to fit together. I felt frustrated, but I knew that time would unravel the full picture. All I could do was go with the flow and grab the opportunities as they came.

Peter was to become one of the most important people in my life over the next few years. Without his insight, encouragement and support I don't think I could have achieved all that I set out to do, or survived many of the trials that were to come our way. I'm deeply grateful for all that he has done.

Shortly after my meeting with Peter, I heard about an American nutritionist and biochemist working in London. I wondered if this could be the American link that had been mentioned. Peter had implied that finding this connection might take years, but I didn't want this to be true. I wanted to compress years into weeks and find the answers now. Henry was now nine and Freddie five, and I was longing to move on to the next stage. I'm one of the world's most impatient people, which on the one hand is good because I get moving and get things done, but on the other hand is incredibly frustrating when things take time.

I made an appointment to see Bob, the American. He had a broad, holistic view of the mechanics of the body which I hadn't encountered before, and he taught me a lot. Intrigued by Henry, Bob felt that he probably had a neuro-transmitter problem – in other words that the neuro-transmitters in his brain weren't passing signals properly. I had already suspected, as a result of my research, that this might be the issue.

But Henry's problems weren't really in Bob's area of expertise – Freddie was the one he felt he might be able to help. He explained that his patients, who were mostly adult, often came to him suffering from acute depression, but that this actually stemmed from a physical problem they might not even have been aware of. His theory was that if you could cure the physical problem the mind would also be cured. He felt that all the physical trauma Freddie had suffered had led to his mental shutdown, and gave us a programme of supplements to bring harmony and balance to the running of his body. The programme included smart drugs known as 'cognitive enhancers' as well as vitamin and mineral supplements.

Bob didn't charge us for the consultations but we had to pay for the supplements and they cost a bomb – about £400 per month. But Michael and I felt the investment was worth it. At the very worst it would do nothing, and at best it might help Freddie. We agreed to give it a few months and see what happened. Bob also suggested we try magnetic field therapy and we booked an appointment with a girl called Chantal who worked in a basement room below his office. The children instantly adored Chantal. She was a gorgeous French girl with the most wonderful heavy accent, and it was love at first sight for Freddie. Over the next few weeks we weren't sure whether Freddie's progress was due to the therapy and supplements or to the delicious Chantal. A few months later, when the Foundation's researcher left, I asked Chantal to take her place. She wanted to spread her wings academically, loved everything alternative and had a good grounding in medicine. She was perfect for it, and to my delight she agreed.

Michael had in the meantime become chairman of a group of art dealers who were setting up an initiative called Asian Art in London. This, they hoped, would pull in more clients on an annual basis for lectures, exhibitions and, most importantly, buying art. Their first event was to be a royal gala dinner at the Victoria and Albert Museum, a grand affair for five hundred people.

Thank goodness I didn't have to help in the organisation of it – one ball was enough for me! The dinner was a very sumptuous affair and I was seated next to Sir James

Weatherall, Marshal of the Diplomatic Corps. He was a cross between Billy Bunter and Tigger, rather round and full of the most incredible energy. Initially I was terrified of him, but to my relief he turned out to be one of the most engaging and charming of men. He was the Queen's representative in dealings with diplomats, and when he mentioned that his offices were in St James's Palace I plucked up courage and rather cheekily asked if we could hold a fundraising party for the Henry Spink Foundation there. He said, 'Yes – ring me in January.' I did, and true to his word he offered us his offices for a party the following March.

The Foundation's office, where our researcher was based, was now set up in the central London premises of Contact a Family. Meanwhile I did all the fundraising from my little office at home. My good friend Alex had agreed to come and type for us – I had no idea how to switch on a computer, let alone use one, so I was grateful for her help. Alex was an extremely attractive blonde and when the opportunity arose we went out to functions together, hoping to network and raise funds for the Foundation. We would home in on people who might be able to help us and we developed a routine. If it was a man, it was pretty easy to discern whether he liked blondes or brunettes. If he liked blondes Alex would dominate the conversation, and if he liked brunettes I would! We had a lot of fun.

Alex knew the ballerina Darcey Bussell's mother and suggested it would be great if Darcey would agree to be our second Patron. Felicity Kendal hadn't been able to come to our Halloween Ball as she'd been performing in the theatre that night, and we thought it would be a good idea to have more celebrities we could call upon. We wrote to Darcey's mother and asked her to talk to Darcey on our behalf. We were elated when Darcey agreed – what a coup to have the country's top prima ballerina on board!

Next we decided to look for a male Patron, but who to choose? After much thought we came up with gardening expert and novelist Alan Titchmarsh. He was perfect – well known, unspoilt and really nice. I rang his agent, Lily Panagi. Lily and I instantly hit it off, but she wouldn't agree to him being Patron; he was far too committed to trillions of other charities, she said, to add another. But I was determined not to give up. I decided to keep up the connection with Lily by inviting her to the St James's Palace party.

Next we thought of Alastair Stewart, the *London Tonight* newsreader. He seemed like another thoroughly nice, popular person. I rang the *London Tonight* office and asked if I could leave a message for him. When they put me through to his office, much to my amazement he picked up the phone himself. He was charming and I hardly knew what to say – I felt like a gushing schoolgirl. I stuttered my request, and the next thing I knew he was inviting me out to lunch. I was far too timid to go alone and asked whether I could bring Michael too, to which he happily agreed. But when the time came I discovered to my horror that Michael had to be abroad. I'm afraid to say courage failed me. I made a very feeble excuse and cancelled lunch with Alastair, which meant that I couldn't ask him to become involved.

Organising the party at the Palace was great fun. Sir

James's office – which was about five times the size of the average drawing room and would easily hold a hundred people – was right next to Prince Charles's and I knew all our guests would love that. Holding the party at St James's Palace – which we soon shortened to SJP – was great value for money. Food, champagne and staff for a hundred guests cost a total of about £600. We decided not to charge for tickets, but to use the event as an opportunity to do some serious networking for the Foundation.

We knew we would have no shortage of people who would want to come, so we set about inviting as many important guests as possible. Debbie Moore, owner of the Pineapple Studios in Covent Garden, had called me after reading about us in the press and had asked if she could become involved in the Foundation. Her daughter had been hit by a terrible condition that had left her unable to walk. Debbie knew what it was like to have suffered enormously over a child and wanted to contribute. I was delighted to welcome her on to the council of the charity and she promised to come to the party. Next I rang Jenni Murray from Radio 4's *Woman's Hour* – she too was delighted to accept.

When the evening of the party arrived we were thrilled with our guest list. They ranged from the wonderful teachers at Henry's school to high-profile celebrities. Everyone had a good evening, and Jim Weatherall generously suggested we book his offices again in the future. Our party showed us what a potentially incredible goldmine SJP could be – with a venue like that we could attract all kinds of people and make lots of money for the

Foundation. I asked Jim whether we could hold a party again that May. He instantly agreed.

This time I set about drumming up a really impressive guest list – I knew this was a real opportunity to get the Foundation known to a wide and influential audience. I rang Alastair Stewart again; I still wanted him on board and felt rather ashamed of my previous cowardly behaviour. Again he picked up the phone himself. Surprisingly he remembered me and I asked him if he'd come to our next party at the Palace. He said he'd come, but only if I had lunch with him first. I promised I would, and this time I kept my promise. At a delightful lunch in one of his favourite Covent Garden restaurants Alastair was warm and friendly and made me feel that what I was talking about mattered.

Next I rang Fergus Walsh, the BBC health correspondent who had presented the feature about us at the time of the Halloween Ball. To my delight he agreed to come, and so did both our Patrons, Felicity Kendal and Darcey Bussell. Buoyed up by success, I decided to try Lily Panagi, Alan Titchmarsh's agent, again. He still wasn't available, she said, but she could come herself and could she bring her mother?

I felt the perfect touch would be the presence of a member of the royal family, but I wasn't sure who to approach. The thought filled me with terror, but I knew that if I could come up with one it would be an extremely smart move. After a lot of thought I decided to approach the Duchess of Gloucester – she was very popular, and contacting her out of the blue didn't feel too terrifying. I asked Sir James about all the formalities that went with approaching a royal and duly sent off my letter. I knew it was a long shot, but figured if you don't ask you don't get. To my astonishment the Duchess replied that she would be happy to come and support the Foundation. This put a whole new slant on the evening. To be able to say we were holding a party at St James's Palace in the presence of royalty was quite a feat. We would have no problem attracting guests. The formalities would be tremendous – but, thank goodness, Sir James was prepared to teach me everything I'd need to know, from curtseying to greetings and introductions.

To begin with Michael, Sir James and I would greet the Duchess with our two Patrons, Darcey and Felicity, and certain members of the council of the charity. Dauntingly, I would then be required, during the course of the evening, formally to introduce every single guest to her. This meant I must know exactly who they were and what they did. Sir James advised me to hold a small card with tiny notes on it discreetly in my hand, just in case I needed to remind myself of any details.

The party was to be held on a Thursday. On the Tuesday before, I received a rather bemused call from Sir James's secretary who said that Felicity Kendal had just turned up and they'd had to send her away, as it was the wrong night. Felicity had looked rather mortified, muttered under her breath and then disappeared. She later told me that she had stopped at the police barrier guarding the entry into St James's Palace and asked the policeman if he would be there on the following Thursday. When he replied 'No' she said, 'Oh good, then I can wear the same frock!'

The evening went without a hitch. I even managed not to stumble once over all the formalities. I wished I had had a camera to record some of it. I remember laughing as Sharon, Henry's teacher, turned up to the party with Freddie's teacher, Tracy. Shaz and Trace at St James's Palace! Everyone had a great time, and I discovered later that quite a few of them nicked some of the loo paper as a souvenir.

Lily was clearly impressed that we had achieved a real royal at the party. She sidled over to me towards the end of the evening and said she thought it would, after all, be a good idea if Alan became one of our Patrons. I'd got my man, even if it had taken two parties at St James's Palace!

Alastair and Fergus, my two TV representatives, had evidently had a good evening and looked very happy. I asked both of them if they would become involved with the Foundation, and both agreed. I asked Fergus to join the council, and Alastair agreed to become our fourth Patron. This gave us two men and two women Patrons, and meant that at least one of them would, with luck, always be available for future events.

At the end of the evening Michael and I accompanied the Duchess to her waiting car. As I gave her my now perfected curtsey, she said she would be delighted to support future events for the Foundation. When she'd gone I whooped with joy. We had royal approval.

Chapter 11

One day early in the summer of 1998 I received a call from my sister Cara to say that our father was not at all well. I had seen him only twice since our wedding. The first time was when he'd come to Henry's christening at the last minute. He had stood at the back of the church and left just before the end so that he wouldn't have to talk to anyone. The next time was when Cara telephoned him with the news of Freddie's birth and suggested he visit his grandson before he died.

Cara had arranged to meet our father at the hospital. Coincidentally Debbie, our then nanny, had also come to visit, with Henry. Debbie and Henry had waited for the lift with my father standing next to them, neither knowing who the other was. When my sister turned up she couldn't stop laughing at the irony of the situation, but my father found it singularly unfunny. By the time he got to my room he had not only met his first grandson but had seen his second on life-support, and he was looking thoroughly traumatised. He brought me some yellow roses and held my hand while I wept. We said very little, and he stayed only a short while.

A couple of weeks later Cara phoned him to ask if he wanted to know that Freddie had survived his operation and was slowly improving. To which my father replied that he didn't want to know, as it was causing him too much suffering and he didn't want to have to think about it.

That was seven years ago. Now, within a week of my receiving the news that he was ill, another call came to say that he had terminal lung and stomach cancer and hadn't got long to live. I gathered that he had been ill for some time and had suppressed the truth from himself and everyone else by drowning the pain in whisky and painkillers. Now, at the relatively young age of sixty, the hour of reckoning had come and the word 'terminal' must have shattered him. How does anyone face death? I can only imagine the anguish that he and his second family must have suffered.

I felt utterly torn. Should I try to see my father and make peace before he died? I knew deep down that he loved me, but our relationship had lapsed through all the years of hurt and distance. He had never been prepared for the utter devastation that resulted when he and my mother divorced and had perhaps behaved childishly towards my mother out of revenge. He had effectively abandoned us, and this had had a terrible effect on Cara and me.

My sister had always been desperate to have him be a proper father. Perhaps she had more memories than I did of our early childhood before he disappeared. All I knew was that it was beyond his capacity to accept us on real terms. I agonised and deliberated. My mother urged me to see him. My father and his wife were now back living in a flat in London, and my sister was seeing him on a daily basis. My mother wanted Cara to organise a meeting and to take my hand and his and reunite us. Perhaps she felt my father and I would regret it if we didn't have a reconciliation at this final hour.

I'm sure my father felt as muddled and uncertain about things as I did. Neither of us knew quite how to get past the hurdle of not having seen one another for so long, let alone cope with his death. I didn't feel I could simply march into his flat and demand to see him. We both needed someone, a generous go-between, to bring us together before he died. But Cara was not willing to be our go-between. She became more and more angry as I hesitated, and in the end she told my mother she didn't want me coming on the scene and confusing things at such a late date. My mother pointed out, firmly but kindly, that when our father was dead Cara would still have a sister with whom she could have shared his last moments. But Cara was firm.

I remember sitting in my bedroom staring out of the window after I heard this news. I went into a kind of semi-trance and I felt my father's presence. I don't know whether I spoke out loud or whether it was the voice within me that spoke, but an inner peace filled me and I said to him, 'Go in peace. We'll sort this out another time. Be free.'

I still wanted my father to see photos of the boys and to understand my hopes and visions for them. I wanted him to know that the disabilities he had so wanted to avoid seeing had enriched my life. It really mattered to me that he knew before he died that I truly believed all would be well.

The next weekend Janet and I drove the boys to

Cornwall while Michael was away in Paris on a business trip. We visited one of our favourite spots on the Cornish coast, Kynance Cove. The cliffs, rugged and awe-inspiring, look as if the hand of God has touched them. The heather covering the craggy scenery was in full bloom and its perfume scented the air. I sat the boys amongst the heather and took photographs with an Instamatic camera. I wanted my father to know that my boys were beautiful and that Henry was the complete image of him. I gathered small wild flowers, took them home and ironed them between sheets of kitchen paper, a quick way of pressing flowers. I felt sure my father would love a sample of nature propped next to his bed as a reminder of all that's beautiful in the world outside. Then I parcelled up my photos with my pressed flowers, now mounted, and wrote a letter, loving him and letting him go. I sent the parcel by registered mail. I couldn't risk it getting lost – this was my final farewell.

My father had an elder sister, Cero, whom I had met only a handful of times. Over the years she had dutifully sent us Christmas presents each year and made the statutory annual telephone call in which she would threaten to come and see us, though she never in fact did. She and my father were terribly close – they had clung together, much as my sister and I had, during their rather turbulent and eccentric upbringing. She telephoned me, and I asked her if my father had received my parcel and if it had mattered to him. She was sure no parcel had been delivered but would check with him. He was now at home, waiting to die. I rang the post office, who assured me it had been delivered. I became desperate; my grief and agony at not being able to see him surfaced and I wept and I wept. Michael suggested that perhaps the janitor of the apartments where my father lived might have taken it in and forgotten to hand it over. We rang the janitor, who remembered the parcel and said yes, he had handed it to my stepmother.

In desperation Michael rang Gerard, Cara's husband. Gerard was very Irish and very determined, and on hearing of the missing parcel he promised that he would make sure it landed on my father's lap. He went round to my father's apartment, retrieved the parcel from a broom cupboard where it had apparently been left and gave it to my father. He loved the flowers and, I hope, felt peaceful after reading my letter. I tried to relay to him that no wrongs had been done that could not be forgiven and undone.

Around this time Douglas, the client of Michael's who had taken us to Cambodia and who had become a good friend, was in England on a short visit. He could see the misery my father's illness was causing, and asked us if we would care to come on holiday to Ibiza for two weeks with him and his family. The boys and Janet were invited too.

He told us he had rented a vast villa in the centre of the island. The house was surrounded by hills and olive groves and boasted endless bedrooms, stunning court-yards and a fabulous swimming pool with a breathtaking panoramic view. This was exactly what we needed in order to get away from the intense emotions that were threatening to drown all of us. But I felt some trepida-tion. Even though I had written a parting letter to my father I guess I still hoped that we might somehow manage to see each other before he died. But deep down I knew this wouldn't happen, so in the end I agreed that a holiday was the best thing.

Ibiza was fantastic and the villa exceeded our expectations. Each of the bedrooms seemed the size of a football pitch, all with lavish bathrooms en suite. Oh, what luxury! Douglas's son was one of the most fantastic Thai cooks – eating his food was truly believing. We quickly came to a great arrangement: we'd wash up if he cooked. Everyone was happy.

Both boys adored being in the swimming pool. I had bought every possible flotation aid for them. We wrapped Freddie in a floating jacket, armbands and rubber ring. The poor boy floated but could hardly move. Within about ten minutes – much to my horror, for I was sure he'd drown – he had dextrously extricated himself from virtually all the aids and was left with only the armbands. Meanwhile Henry, wrapped in the same floating armour, had relaxed to such a degree that he had fallen asleep bobbing around in the pool. I removed Freddie from the pool in order to put his jacket on again, but he wriggled straight off my lap and shot off at high speed, bottom-shuffling towards the pool and shouting, 'Again, again.' The silence that followed was immeasurable – time stood still and everyone stared. Freddie had said his very first word. He was almost seven years of age and I'd virtually given up on ever hearing him speak.

None of us knew what to say. How do you celebrate something so momentous? There had been many times when Freddie's steadfast refusal to communicate left us baffled and enraged. It was obvious that he was incredibly bright, but also that his brightness was somehow trapped. It was as though he was hiding behind some unseen barrier, teasing us but never delivering. We knew he was capable of communicating but he absolutely wouldn't. And Freddie was stubborn – once he'd made up his mind not to do something he would rather die than do it. Now, after all our efforts, a bloody swimming pool had got him to speak. I didn't know whether to laugh or cry.

After this it was as though the ice was broken and Freddie was prepared to speak, but only when words slipped out or were an absolute necessity to gain something he wanted. His great passion was music, which he pronounced 'mubik'. Janet and I would only put music on if Freddie agreed to say 'mubik'. I couldn't believe the lengths to which he'd go to resist saying it, even though he was utterly desperate to hear some piece of music. He'd remain furiously silent for hours before relenting with a rather gruff 'mubik' which would be muttered under his breath. He hated communicating with speech – it seemed to invade his private world and bring him closer to the real world he so evidently wished to avoid. But slowly, slowly he was opening up. It was as if he was, mostly against his will, beginning to join us more. We revelled in it.

We swam every day of the holiday – the freedom of the water was a real release for both children. For Henry it must have been bliss. Not only was it luxuriously warm but it lifted the terrible weight of his floppy body – gravity no longer weighed him down.

One day Janet and I had got both boys into the pool and were busy splashing each other. Freddie was giggling away at our antics, though Henry was not amused – he hated being splashed. Michael came up the stairs and walked round the side of the pool to where I was. He said, 'I'm so very sorry. Your father has just died.' Shaking like a leaf, I handed him Freddie and grabbed a towel. Despite all that had happened I couldn't believe my father had left without seeing me. I ran down to the bottom of the hill next to the tennis court in order to shed my tears of anguish and agony in solitude – this was not a moment I wanted to share. There is no solace that can be given in those first few devastating moments of tragedy.

When we thought Freddie was dying I had felt trapped in my grief and Jenny, one of his godparents, had told me I should go to the top of a mountain and scream to release all the trauma I'd been through. I had laughed and said I wasn't a screamer. Several years later I came across a box in my cupboard containing the hundreds of letters I'd received in hospital. As I sat on the bed and started to read, the memories came flooding back and unleashed my pent-up emotions. I wept from the heart as I had never wept before. Now I was weeping again in the same way. I wept for something that could now never be: the relationship my father and I would never have. The dream was over.

I felt a terrible fear that he would suffer for the way he'd behaved towards us. I had forgiven him, and I wanted God to do so as well. Enough suffering had taken place. That night Douglas had organised a dinner party for about twenty guests. I didn't know whether to join in and pretend everything was fine or hide away in my room. In the end I decided to go, and made Douglas promise that he wouldn't mention my father's death to anyone that night. The evening was surreal – I felt out of place. Externally I was smiling, but inside I was frozen in silent grief. I hadn't realised how important it was to me to see my father before he went. I wished my sister had wanted me to share that moment with her. I felt I had lost both my father and my sister.

The rest of the holiday passed in rather a blur. I didn't see much point in going back for the funeral. I'd not been welcome in his last weeks: was there much point in saying goodbye to a coffin? I decided that on the day of his funeral I would find a spot on top of a mountain to lay some flowers, light a candle and say a prayer of farewell to him. I would celebrate his life and offer my prayers as a parting gift, but I would do it alone, untroubled by family divisions.

Two days after my father died, Michael's granny died; and two days after that Douglas's adopted son Piac's wife Pranny's mother died. We all returned to England suntanned but subdued. The elation of hearing Freddie say his first word was the only really happy souvenir of the trip.

I heard from my aunt Maggie that the funeral had been a nightmare. No one had been invited and the location and date had not been made widely known, offending and upsetting many relatives and friends. My aunt, whose lack of subtlety often left you wanting to giggle, told me, 'There were about fifteen people, including David in his coffin.' She described how after the funeral they'd all traipsed into the vestry for tea and buns, my stepmother greeting each guest as they entered. My father was to be cremated and my aunt enquired if they were to accompany my father to the crematorium. The gruff reply was that he would come back in a pot after tea! I was deeply grateful I had not been there.

My father left nothing to me or to Cara. My sister was devastated and got copies of his will from Somerset House to see whether it was true. I hadn't thought about it much and didn't expect anything. I suppose that for Cara being left nothing was the end of the long-held dream that he might come through for us. I think I had let go of that particular dream a long time before. A memento of him would have been nice, but I settled for a pocketful of shadowy memories.

Since we still had two weeks of the summer holiday left we had decided to go to the cottage in Cornwall. Both boys had grown and were looking healthy and tanned. Henry's muscle tone had slightly improved – perhaps the swimming in Ibiza had stimulated some unreachable part of his brain. It certainly appeared to have done so with Freddie.

A few days into the holiday we'd spent a busy morning with the boys collecting cockles, which both children adored eating with butter and garlic. That afternoon we'd collapsed in front of a video. I was fiddling with a video camera Douglas had bought us as a present, while Janet had Henry on her lap and Michael was reading a newspaper. Suddenly Freddie got to his feet and staggered across the room. He managed about twelve feet before collapsing into an armchair. Michael, Janet and I sat in stunned silence. Freddie grinned and squealed with delight. 'Again, again,' he shouted, and staggered back across the room. His smile was the biggest I've ever seen. Through sheer luck I caught this magical moment on video. Freddie had walked.

Chapter 12

On the strength of the funds we had raised I had been able to employ two more staff to work for the Foundation, Jill and Suzy. They were based in our office with Chantal, but Suzy was also helping me on the fundraising side. So far I had been doing all the fundraising alone and it was a heavy responsibility. I was glad of another pair of hands.

In the weeks after my father's death I was busy organising a concert to raise funds for the Foundation while trying rather unsuccessfully to distract myself from my misery over the fact that my sister and I weren't speaking. We had already organised a classical concert at Christie's, which had sold out instantly. This time we were going to have an Indian theme, with poetry readings in Persian, and the concert would be at Spink and Son. Michael's cousin Anthony, who was Chairman, had kindly offered us the use of the main galleries on the ground floor. I hoped the subject wouldn't be too obscure and that people would enjoy something so diverse and exotic. It was fun to be able to offer a more challenging programme – but only if the tickets sold!

Throwing my energy into organising the concert did me good. I really enjoyed it and it was a great success, and we had instant demands for a repeat. But that night, as we returned home afterwards, we found that, not for the first time, someone had parked in our disabled bay. There was nothing we could do, and this would make getting the kids into the car next morning a nightmare. I was so angry I grabbed some of the children's coloured poster paints, which happened to come in handy squeezy bottles. Armed with three bright colours, I squirted paint all around the top rim of the car and watched with enormous satisfaction as it dripped down the sides in glorious multi-coloured stripes. Later that night our neighbours passed by and we could hear howls of laughter as they screeched, 'Glad we didn't park there!' Next morning the offending driver revved his car in fury and sped off. I noted that the supposedly washable paint didn't begin to fade from the pavement for a full three weeks, and hoped it had been the same with the car.

Janet, our nanny, had meanwhile met a young man who seemed rather obsessive by nature. Perhaps he was jealous of Janet's closeness to us – I shall never know. But he appeared to want to remove her as quickly as possible, and Janet announced that she was leaving. Of course we always knew that she would move on at some point, but her sudden and dramatic departure felt like a real blow. She left only two months after my father's death and I felt my heart would break. Janet was my lifeline, my friend and a surrogate mother to the boys, particularly to Freddie. He was devastated at her departure, and there was nothing I could do to lessen his pain.

We had no time to organise a replacement before Michael flew to Singapore to give a lecture and a live TV performance. He couldn't possibly miss it, but it meant that I was left alone with the children over half-term with no support. We advertised for a special needs nanny, but no one applied for the job. When the boys were babies finding nannies had been easier, but most nannies were far less keen on caring for older disabled children. Eventually we gave up placing ads and tried agencies. Over the next few months we had a succession of girls, each of whom appeared to have more problems than the last. On one occasion a homesick girl left us two days after the agency trial period ran out, which meant we lost our £600 fee and had no help either.

Until Janet's departure Freddie had been getting along fine with my mother at St Joseph's. Janet had taken and collected him every day and all had been going well. But the upheaval of her leaving and the quick-fire nanny changes which followed left him unsettled, and we were forced to recognise that the school was no longer able to provide what he needed.

It was obvious to everyone by now, including us, that Freddie too had profound special needs, even though we still hadn't approached any specialists for a diagnosis. The boys were very different in their disabilities, but despite this we still believed that Freddie was probably suffering from a lesser version of whatever ailed Henry, with a few extra complications such as the diaphragmatic hernia thrown in. Freddie was making some progress – he did walk, though a little stiffly and unsteadily, and he was beginning to speak a little, but his ability level was a very long way behind that of his classmates. He couldn't read or write or concentrate on a game or task. We had to face up to the fact that a mainstream nursery was no longer the right environment for him.

We contacted Wandsworth council's special needs education department and were assigned a case-worker, who had an assessment of Freddie's needs done in record time. We were told that the only school available to meet his needs was Paddock, to which we had steadfastly refused to send Henry. We found Paddock unprepossessing and our hearts sank. Henry's school, Greenmead, was much more pleasant, but was for physically handicapped children, while Paddock was for children who were mobile but mentally disabled. We spoke to the head teacher of Greenmead, Angela Laxton, about sending Freddie there with Henry, but she felt that it wouldn't be good for Freddie to be one of the only mobile children in the school and we knew she was right.

So we chose Paddock and Freddie started there in January, two months after his seventh birthday. We decided Michael would accompany him for the first few days to settle him. Freddie was very attached to me, and we knew that if I were the one who took him he might refuse to stay and there would be stress all round. Freddie's teacher turned out to be terrific, and he soon settled. But starting him at Paddock was an emotional blow to us. It was as if his disabilities, so long denied, were suddenly right in our faces. I felt there was absolutely no aspect of our lives that was normal.

Cornwall was our one place of sanctuary, a timely gift from God which was keeping us sane. There we could briefly escape the hardships of life and other people's opinions and just be ourselves. We were hugely grateful for this as we struggled to come to terms with Freddie's condition.

On top of everything else, we had financial worries. A year earlier Michael had left Spink and Son. They had been bought out by Christie's and had invited Michael to be senior fine art director. But by early 1998 the writing was on the wall: it was clear that Christie's would close Spink and Son and Michael decided to leave before this happened. Since then he'd been self-employed, but business wasn't too good. Times were changing, and so were attitudes towards buying and selling antiques. Collecting expensive art was becoming a thing of the past. Few new collectors were appearing, and the old ones were either dying off or had completed their collections. During the eighties the prices, particularly in the Islamic art market, had risen so high that many middle-level dealers and collectors had been knocked out and they had never returned. The circle of dealers and collectors buying Islamic art was shrinking fast.

Now, to make things even worse, the government was planning to introduce legislation that would effectively ban the movement and sale of antiquities. Everyone in the art market was aware that temples and archaeological sites were being looted, but the new laws, if they came into force, would stop virtually all forms of art movement, both legitimate and illegitimate. The climate in the world of art dealing was very uncertain.

The knock-on effect of all this was that Michael's income was reduced. We still had a little money left over from our wonderful win, but it was disappearing rapidly on the cost of the boys' care.

Now that we had both boys in school I was free for the first time in eleven years during school hours. Freddie had only ever attended my mother's nursery class during the mornings, so finding myself with a full six-hour day was a whole new experience. The cooking, extra cleaning and endless laundry still had to be done, but I could devote a couple of hours to these each morning and then work for the Foundation until school finished in the afternoon.

This meant we didn't need childcare for so many hours, but I still needed another pair of hands to help feed the children morning and night. Neither fed himself. Henry didn't have the coordination to do it and Freddie had decided he wouldn't. We knew he could because he'd happily fed himself little yogurts when he was only ten months old. But not long after that, when his vomiting was at its worst, he had stopped feeding himself. It was almost as if he had watched Henry and decided to be like him.

We decided to forget about nannies and try for an au pair. Eventually I found an agency who said they didn't usually deal with special needs but happened to have a twenty-eight-year-old Slovenian girl who was keen to do this. Her name was Velma and her English was lousy, but she was warm and kind and seemed willing. Velma was petite and wiry, with very black hair and bright blue eyes. She had a nice sense of humour and didn't complain about lifting the boys at all. But there was one major hiccup – she had plainly never been taught about personal hygiene. She stayed with us for six months, during which she took only a handful of baths. I left soap and deodorant in her bathroom, opened the car windows in midwinter and tried every other hint I could think of. Nothing worked, and I was too embarrassed to tackle her directly. Velma explained that she had never travelled outside Slovenia before and had never seen a black person. Now that she was in London, with its very cosmopolitan racial mix, she clearly intended to make up for lost time and soon developed a fixation with black men in Peckham. We never could work out why Peckham, but Velma would head there every weekend.

One Sunday evening Michael and I and the boys were curled up on the sofa watching a video when she arrived back. Freddie bounced up off the sofa to rush over and greet her – and instantly recoiled. The stench of body odour, old sex and fags was too much even for Freddie.

Not only did Velma not believe in the use of soap, but it soon became clear that contraceptives were on her list of no-gos too. One morning she announced that she thought she was pregnant and needed to get hold of the morning-after pill. I didn't feel it was my place to lecture so I dutifully dropped her off at an NHS walk-in centre, hoping they would advise her on the use of precautions. Not so, and Velma soon became a regular at the walk-in centre, where morning-after pills would be handed over with no questions asked.

She came to Cornwall with us for the Easter break. It was nice to have the extra pair of hands, but we couldn't leave the boys with her and so were never able to have a break. It took two very competent and responsible people to manage both boys. In London we occasionally went out, leaving Velma in charge, once the boys were in bed. But in Cornwall the cottage was just too isolated for that.

On our return from Cornwall I was somewhat surprised to find Velma in a real state. It turned out that she was pregnant. Tucked away in our corner of Cornwall she had been far from any walk-in clinic, and now it was too late for any pill to help. Michael and I had put the boys to bed that night and gone to the cinema for a much-needed break. We returned to find a fraught Velma sitting in the hallway with her bags packed and a taxi just arriving outside. She had planned to bolt, leaving the boys alone until we got back. She departed, presumably to have her baby back in Slovenia. And that was the last we heard of her.

Numbness began to descend over both of us. Would we never have decent help again? We'd been incredibly fortunate to have eleven years of marvellous, reliable and friendly help from Debbie, Angela, Jodie and Janet, but things had now gone badly wrong. We'd dealt with so many problems we could hardly bear to imagine what might hit us next. Angela had remained a close friend and often came over at weekends to see the boys. Occasionally she would corner my mother and cajole her into helping for a weekend so that Michael and I could get away together. Angela was one of those hugely energetic people who would do a day job, spend the evening studying for her law degree and then do a night job after that, sleeping only four hours before the cycle began again. She kept this up for four years, often seven days a week.

I had huge respect for her. Her determination to

succeed and become a lawyer in a foreign country was incredible. There was no doubt in our minds that she would succeed. And despite her punishing schedule she still wanted to have the boys and give us the odd break. She managed this about once a year, and it made the world of difference to us. Those forty-eight hours each year were our lifeline, a brief chance to be a couple again and not just the parents of two disabled boys.

Angela never wanted to be paid – her love and generosity were far too great to want anything in return. She was the only person who realised that Michael and I, although we loved the boys with every fibre of our being, still needed a break. Other people around us seemed unaware of this and of the fact that we were coping with children who needed twenty-four-hour care. Simple privileges that many other people take for granted, such as dropping the kids off with a friend or relative for a few days, were never possible for us and the result was that we felt very alone. During the years where we had good, supportive nannies things had felt a little easier. But now, left with no help or the occasional inadequate, problematic au pair, we began to feel the full force of the absence of outside help.

The boys were getting bigger. Freddie was almost eight and Henry would soon be twelve. It was getting harder to lift them and we knew we would soon need equipment, as well as more pairs of hands. We were both becoming increasingly tired and worn down. Henry still wouldn't sleep through the night and, though he woke less often than when he was small, we were still up with him at least three times a night. Life felt like an endurance test which would never end, and we both felt low. No one seemed to care, and it hurt.

Shortly after acknowledging to ourselves that we needed more help, Sarah, one of the lovely occupational therapists from Henry's school, approached me out of the blue and suggested that she came and did an assessment, as Henry was fast approaching the 'heavy lifting category'. I was delighted. I had never known what kind of equipment we might be entitled to – largely because everyone we asked refused to tell us. We had been given one or two previous OT (occupational therapy) assessments, but the only things we had received free in twelve years were two specially adapted plastic drinking mugs. When one of these mugs had broken we had been refused a replacement and had eventually been given an old one which had belonged to a boy at school who had died. No sensitivity there.

In due course Sarah came and did a formal assessment. Ours was a typical London house on five floors with lots of stairs. We were still carrying both boys up and down the long flights, as we had always done. Although Freddie could walk a little, his stiffness prevented him from climbing stairs. When Sarah suggested we have stair lifts installed something inside me sagged with relief. The prospect of not having to cart the boys up and down any more released a wave of exhaustion in me. She also mentioned a bath seat to lift Henry in and out of the bath.

When I asked her how the process worked I was taken aback by her response. She now had to do the assessment all over again in the presence of a senior Wandsworth occupational therapist. We contacted the council – the earliest slot they had was in twelve weeks. I was disappointed that we had to wait so long, but cheered to think that after that we would get help.

When the twelve weeks had passed, Sue, the senior OT, came round to watch Sarah assess the situation again. Sarah hammed it up and got the message across that we needed stair lifts. I was over the moon when Sue agreed that it was 'unsafe and dangerous' for us to continue lifting the boys. I assumed Sue would sign off the order and stair lifts would then be installed. How naïve I was! She laughed nervously and said her assessment of Sarah's assessment would now have to be assessed by Wandsworth's finance department; it would be means tested and take up to two years. I gasped. The idea of waiting so long seemed horrific. The boys would be fourteen and ten by then, and both were becoming rapidly heavier. And we had no spare cash to contribute. The last of our pools win had now gone, eaten up by the cost of caring for the boys.

A few weeks later it was time for Henry's annual school review. He had stayed at Greenmead for an extra year, as both Michael and I felt he would benefit from it, but now it was time to discuss his transition to secondary school. During the meeting Henry's educational psychologist made notes as we spelled out his needs – a quiet environment and one-to-one support, which he had never had. Angela Laxton, the head teacher, confirmed that Greenmead was now unable to meet Henry's needs and that he needed the extra support of a personal assistant to enable him to access the curriculum fully.

There were two possible schools for Henry to move on to. The first was Paddock, where Freddie was, which we already knew was completely unsuitable for Henry. The other choice was a school called Bedelsford, in the neighbouring borough of Kingston. Four of Henry's class, with whom he'd spent eight years, had gone on to Bedelsford and were extremely happy there. We felt this school sounded right for Henry too. A friend of ours, Sue, had a son called Albert who had been with Henry since they were tiny. Albert was a year older than Henry and had gone to Bedelsford the year before and Sue thoroughly recommended it.

A few months earlier Wandsworth had threatened to close Greenmead and an adjoining special needs school for delicate children. They had discovered that, if sold, the site was worth £10 million. Uproar ensued, and Wandsworth was faced with a barrage of very angry parents all fighting to save their school. Unfortunately for the council that year's parents were a vociferous and articulate bunch, and the plans were thwarted. Angela Laxton had warned us at the time that being involved in the fight to keep Greenmead open might jeopardise Henry's transition to his next school. Wandsworth could make things awkward if they so wished. But we felt we had no choice – we had to fight to save this marvellous school. We couldn't believe that Wandsworth, however annoyed by the protests, would deny a vulnerable child the education he needed.

After the meeting with Henry's head teacher and educational psychologist we looked at both schools, knowing full well which one met Henry's needs. We instantly loved Bedelsford; it was a natural follow-on from Greenmead and would take the same educational approach, besides which four of his classmates would be there to welcome him. The head teacher offered Henry a place and we felt relieved and happy. We informed Wandsworth of our choice and waited to receive confirmation that we could go ahead.

A couple of weeks later we received a letter from Wandsworth regarding the stair lifts. The contents left me reeling. They had decided that Henry could not have a stair lift as he could not operate it himself. Further to this ludicrous comment they also stated:

2. stair lifts are not provided for children with multiple handicaps
3. stair lifts are only provided for people who can use them independently
4. stair lifts are not provided for people with poor sitting or standing balance
5. stair lifts are not provided for people with epilepsy.

In other words, you had to be physically able to get one. These criteria certainly must have saved the council a bit of money.

I felt that Wandsworth had made up the ludicrous guidelines excluding Henry from having a stair lift. They used the ploy of offering an alternative which was wholly unsuitable – a massive great lift shaft that they wanted to install in the middle of our drawing room, straight through the ceiling into the middle of our bedroom. This folly of an architectural design would make our house completely unsaleable – I'm sure they banked on this and knew we would refuse. Oh . . . and we would have to pay for the lift anyway, which would cost far more than the stair lift. As a result Wandsworth cleverly said they had offered us something and that we had rejected it. Case closed.

We were also told we could not have the bath seat that the occupational therapist had recommended, again on the basis that Henry couldn't operate it himself. Instead we were offered a disabled walk-in shower which would replace our bath. The bath seat would have cost £600, whereas the shower cost £7,000 and we would have to pay for it ourselves. Even if we could have afforded it and managed with no bath, there was still the small issue of Henry, who hated showers and had a fit whenever one was turned on. Wandsworth's conclusion was that we 'should move house' and I 'should continue to lift Henry'. I'd love to know where they thought we should move to – there aren't too many bungalows in Battersea.

I immediately rang them and demanded to speak to someone in charge. I asked if I could apply to have a stair lift myself: I could operate it, had good balance and didn't suffer from any multi-disability or have epilepsy. I said I thought their letter so ridiculous that it deserved printing in the national press. This was complete bravado on my part, but worth throwing in just for the hell of it. After a sour 'No, you cannot apply for a stair lift' they hung up.

The only thing we got – eventually, as the result of a visit by another occupational therapist – was a loo seat. I had not even known until this point that such a seat existed, let alone that we might be entitled to one. Every night for twelve years, I had held a very wriggly Henry on the loo for an hour or so. This was appallingly difficult, and looking back I don't know how I survived it. The new seat changed our lives. Instead of forcibly holding Henry to prevent him from falling off I could now sit on a chair next to him and read to him.

We ended up buying the bath seat ourselves, and it worked just fine. When, a couple of years later, we needed a second bath seat for the house in Cornwall, another, very nice, OT said we could get round the issue of not being able to get one on account of Henry not being able to operate it by applying for one for Freddie, who didn't really need it but could operate it. This meant we were able to take our first bath seat to Cornwall and Henry borrowed 'Freddie's' when we were in London.

After Wandsworth's patronising and ridiculous letter I decided to write a long, detailed and, I hoped, humorous letter to various members of the Houses of Lords and Commons, outlining the stupid battles we'd had to endure on behalf of our children over the years. Perhaps someone in power would stop this nonsense. I began with our fight for a disabled parking space. We had urgently needed a disabled bay outside the house to get our two non-walking children in and out of the car. We finally got a registered bay by the time they were four and seven. Problem solved? No! Anyone with an orange disabled badge could park in our space and, on a crowded London street, of course they did. I told the council the space was useless unless it was personalised. They said our borough did not offer this service – although some others did. When I told them I just couldn't cope unless they helped, they told me to take it up with the government.

My next point was a serious grouse about wheelchair

policies. At school, Henry needed a wheelchair for seating, rather than transport, purposes. This wheelchair was narrow and very difficult to push, as you constantly caught your feet on the wheels. We therefore needed a second wheelchair for him to use out of school. We were told that we could apply to go on a voucher scheme which would allow us to purchase the wheelchair of our choice. We decided that a three-wheeler all-terrain buggy would suit his needs and allow us the freedom to go for walks and explore new places with Henry.

At first we were just told we couldn't have it, without explanation. Then we were told yes, we could have it, but that the scheme only entitled us to one wheelchair, so the school one would be taken away. They added that the voucher would cover only half the cost of the buggy, that it should last five years and that we would be responsible for all repairs.

This was impossible. Henry was nearly twelve and on the verge of a growth spurt – he would need to have his seating reassessed well before he reached his seventeenth birthday. And he needed both the school and the outdoor wheelchairs. This scheme seemed to be a con, leading parents to believe they could have some say in choosing a suitable chair and then allowing the council to escape the tedious responsibilities of maintenance, health and safety.

I prattled on for page after page, fed up with the idiotic rules which seemed to be designed to mock our predicament and blight our lives. I filled in the story of the stair lift and the bath seat and ended with what must be the most ridiculous example of bureaucratic madness – the nappy saga. Henry was incontinent and needed nappies at all times. I had discovered that if you're lucky enough to live in Surrey, you are entitled to ten packets of nappies a month. In Clapham you get seven and in Battersea a whopping two. Do they know something I don't? Do city children crap less than their country cousins?

By the time I'd finished I felt proud of my letter and hoped that someone, somewhere, would take note. By chance later that day I was chatting to a friend, Elizabeth, Lady Astor of Hever. Elizabeth had an autistic daughter and was on the council of my charity, lending it much-needed glamour and grandeur. I told her about the stair lift saga and she suggested I ring Cassandra Jardine at the *Daily Telegraph*, a very nice journalist who had just written a feature on her and her daughter.

I decided to call. Cassandra picked up the phone and kindly listened to my story. I mentioned that I had written it all up in a letter which I had sent off to various politicians. She asked me to fax it over and rang me straight back, agreeing to run a feature on it. I grinned – what would Wandsworth make of that?

Chapter 13

Excited about Cassandra's feature, I hoped it would show up all the ridiculous bureaucracy we had to deal with. All I wanted was to get my kids up the stairs without breaking my back. It didn't seem so much to ask. I naïvely thought that a politician or two might be aghast at such appallingly ridiculous treatment and step forward to protest. Not so. No one in authority batted an eyelid. I was disappointed.

But if those in authority didn't care, the public certainly did. The day after the article appeared the letters started pouring in. Most of them were from people staggered at what we were going through, some offered help and others told their own stories of misery at the hands of local authorities. I wrote back to every one of them. Michael received a call from Nina Campbell, the interior designer. She told him that a close friend of hers, the author Wilbur Smith, had sadly lost his wife recently after an illness. He had two spare stair lifts still in their wrappings – would we like them? God sure works in mysterious ways! Freddie was thrilled when they were installed and insisted that Winnie the Pooh rode up and down all night. At that stage I wondered how much of a blessing they were actually going to be! But a blessing they certainly were. My life changed overnight. It was heaven not having to carry the boys any more – I hadn't realised what a toll twelve years of strenuous carrying was taking on my health.

Despite Wandsworth's injunctions that children like Henry should not use stair lifts, he was absolutely fine on them. He sat calmly in the chair while we operated the manual control. Freddie could operate the lift himself, which he did with great regularity. Occasionally, when it all got too much for us hearing the slow grind of the stair lift travelling up and down at three in the morning, we'd remove the keys for a bit of peace and quiet – much to Freddie's annoyance. Amongst the correspondence I received a warm letter and a donation from Victoria Getty, Sir Paul's wife. She loved the work I was doing with the Foundation and wanted to offer her support. I decided to invite her to our next party to see if I could tempt her to join the council of the charity.

The response to Cassandra's feature warmed our hearts. It was good to know that there were so many generous and loving souls out there. Having disabled children shows you both the best and the worst in other people, and for every miserable block or cruel, thought-less comment we had received there was someone whose gesture or kind words lifted our spirits. Little did we know at this stage, early in the year 2000, that the response to the feature was to be like a balmy day before the arrival of a hurricane. What was in store for us over the next year was worse by a long stretch than any of the nightmares we had suffered so far.

Henry was twelve and due to move to secondary school. Freddie was eight and making slow but steady progress. But for us and both the boys life was to become infinitely more difficult and challenging over the months to come. As an avalanche of bureaucratic stone walls and cruel injunctions over Henry's education hit us, Freddie's health was simultaneously to leave us in a permanent state of fear and dread. Looking back, I'm glad I didn't know what was to come. How can you prepare yourself for a living hell? As it was, as each new step of the nightmare hit us, we simply gritted our teeth and coped as best we could.

In the toughest moments my faith that ultimately all would be well for my boys, and my vision for them, kept me going. Although there were times when I felt this faith was a burden, and that without it I might have given up and put the boys in care or accepted less than they deserved for the sake of an easier life, ultimately it was a blessing. My faith kept me fighting, searching and refusing to be fobbed off.

The wonderful nannies we'd had in the early years had helped a great deal. We saw that there were people who truly loved and understood our boys. My taped diaries also helped. When things were bad I was able to let off steam and articulate my concerns to a tape recorder, which listened patiently and recorded faithfully.

Humour was the best antidote of all. Thank goodness Michael and I had never lost our deep and loving connection to one another or our ability to find something to laugh about, even at the worst of moments. Our journey, no matter how good or how bad – and believe me, we experienced both in abundance – was a journey we had chosen to make together, and we both held fast to that and to each other when the storms hit.

We always tried to find a counter-balance to the tough times and to the harder aspects of our lives. Every Wednesday, with whichever nanny we had at the time, I would take the boys to the National Gallery to listen to concerts given by students of the Royal College of Music. Both our children had a relationship with music that I cannot even begin to put into words – it was as if it carried them to a different place altogether. The joy I felt, watching their enraptured little faces, was truly wonderful. These concerts were the only times that Freddie could sit completely entranced for an hour and half without moving a muscle.

There were few activities that we didn't try, either. Henry could be a little pansyish, so we'd make him try something and if he really didn't like it then we'd stop. He roared his way in fury round the rollercoaster at Legoland – that was definitely a no-no. But there were other activities he loved, and Freddie was always happy to give things a go.

When we were given a present of two plastic sledges we were determined to use them, despite the fact that neither child could walk and that lugging them back up the slopes would probably kill us. The minute snow fell we set off for the park and got up to the highest slope we could reach. It was wonderful watching the pleasure in Henry's face as he whizzed down the hill and the cold air caressed his face. Both boys loved it, and though we wore ourselves out trailing them back up each time it was a magical day. Moments like this kept my spirit alive. I remained certain that, if I could only keep on track, taking each new step as it came, then I would not only survive, but triumph, by finding the answers my boys needed.

Peter, my psychic healer friend, helped too. At those times when I felt like giving up, he urged me on with his special blend of insight and encouragement. He warned me about a lot of what was to come, though I didn't always understand or take in what he said. But, more importantly, he helped me to believe that I would come through it all and survive.

The first indication we had of the battle that was to come over Henry's education was when Angela Laxton, the head teacher at his school, rang us to say that his draft statement had come back from Wandsworth's education department. This was an assessment of our child's needs in secondary education, specifying, for instance, that Henry would need speech therapy, physiotherapy and so on. The draft statement is pretty much a discussion document, and the name of the proposed secondary school is not usually mentioned. The final statement is issued eight weeks after the draft statement, and this is when the secondary school is named and the provision required by the child is specified.

However, our case was clearly not going to follow the rules. Henry's draft statement named Paddock as the secondary school he would attend. Angela told us that Henry's draft statement was the only one which named the school: the statements for all the other children moving on to secondary school, which had arrived in a batch with Henry's, did not do so. In addition, Henry's statement did not give him a single ounce of specified provision even though his educational psychologist had noted that he needed one-to-one support.

I had no idea what to do. Wandsworth plainly did not have Henry's best interests at heart. They had made up their minds that he would go to Paddock, and his needs as well as the opinions of experts and his parents were to be denied. In order to justify sending him to Paddock Wandsworth had to reclassify Henry. For the past twelve years he had been classified as physically disabled, and educated accordingly. Now suddenly they had decided he was predominantly mentally disabled so that he would fit the Paddock criteria. We were furious. We had read the Education Act, and it clearly stated that parents had a right to choose a school, subject to three criteria. These were: that the child was given a place, that the child fitted in with the other children in the classroom, and that the choice involved 'the efficient use of recourses', i.e. money.

The first two criteria were met – Henry had been offered a place at Bedelsford and would certainly fit in, since many of his old classmates were already there. The sticking point was obviously money. Yet the other Greenmead children had been allowed to move on to Bedelsford – it simply didn't make sense that these children could go and Henry couldn't. Our views had been discounted, and we felt demeaned and humiliated. All we were trying to do was to send our child to a secondary school that would be right for him and meet his needs. The officials who had made the decision about Henry had never met him – to them he was just a statistic on a piece of paper. Yet we, who spent twenty-four hours a day caring for him and knew his needs better than anyone else, were to be ignored and, as we soon discovered, labelled nuisances.

Bedelsford School too had received a letter from Wandsworth, saying that Henry could have a place at the school as long as Bedelsford would cover the cost of his one-to-one support for thirty hours per week. The children at Bedelsford came from ten surrounding boroughs and all had one-to-one support assistants paid for by their local boroughs. Only Wandsworth refused this support. Jamie and Albert, the two other Wandsworth boys already at the school, also needed one-to-one support and had none, so John Murfitt, the head teacher, suggested a compromise to Wandsworth. Would they allow just one classroom assistant, who, instead of giving one boy the thirty hours required, could at least give Jamie, Albert and Henry ten hours each. He argued that one assistant's salary divided by three would be far cheaper in the long run than getting two part-timers, which was the proposed solution for Jamie and Albert. Wandsworth refused.

We weighed up our options. To go to a tribunal, which was the only way to fight our case, would cost us thousands. Support for Henry for ten hours a week would cost £4,000 a year. If it meant Henry could go to Bedelsford we would somehow find the money. We put our offer to Wandsworth – we would pay for the ten hours' support if he could go to Bedelsford. Wandsworth refused. John Murfitt wrote a letter imploring Wandsworth to accept our offer. Wandsworth refused.

Meanwhile Henry's final statement had still not appeared. The borough's education code of practice states that it should be issued eight weeks after the January draft statement, so that if the parents don't agree with the choice of school there is still plenty of time to resolve things before the end of the summer term. Although we knew the school they intended Henry to go to, we couldn't begin to fight back or go to tribunal until this final statement was issued. The statement finally appeared twenty-two weeks after the draft statement. This delay guaranteed that the tribunal hearing would not take place until after the start of the September term, and Henry would be left with no school to go to until the case was resolved. Wandsworth obviously hoped that the delay would pressurise us into accepting Paddock. Meanwhile, Wandsworth wrote to us apologising for the delay in producing the statement and blaming staff shortages. This apology pre-empted any complaint we might have lodged and rendered any form of redress useless.

So far Wandsworth's argument for blocking Henry from going to Bedelsford had been the cost of one-to-one support. But we had offered to pay for the support, so this argument was defunct. Out of the blue they came up with another, and it took us completely by surprise. Now it was the comparative cost of the schools which was the problem. Michael had a meeting with Wandsworth at which he was told that the cost of Bedelsford would be £14,250 a year, while Paddock would only cost £10,096. Wandsworth could legitimately turn us down, because the out-of-borough school cost over £1,000 more than the in-borough school.

This was based on a recent ruling in the House of Lords stating that, if a parent wanted an out-of-borough school, it could cost no more than £1,000 more than the in-borough school. It appeared that Henry was being barred from appropriate education because of a figure plucked out of the air by some bozo in the Lords who had probably sent their own child to an expensive private school. The year after our battle over Henry's education, this ruling was overturned, but not before it had made our lives absolute hell.

Our only choice now was to go to the tribunal to prove that Paddock could not meet Henry's needs. How were we going to do this?

Meanwhile, Angela Laxton was visibly upset by the way we were being treated and offered to keep Henry at Greenmead until the tribunal was over, reorganising the classes to fit him in again. I breathed a deep sigh of relief. I'd wondered how I would manage to balance having Henry out of school with trying to run the charity.

The last party I had given at St James's Palace had netted me a contract with Maiden Outdoor, the poster site group, who had offered us a free poster campaign across London for the next autumn. I needed a great deal of time to organise this. An international competition to design our poster would be held amongst the design colleges and a team of judges, including me, would choose a winner. That poster, advertising our helpline and services, would then be displayed across London. I hoped that a poster campaign would launch us into a different category; it was exciting and daunting at the same time. I was also still raising the funds for the salaries of our three staff and the costs of running the Foundation. It was a huge responsibility, and one I couldn't easily back out of or hand to someone else.

I was quite happy to drive Henry to and from Greenmead while he was still there, but Angela felt that Wandsworth should continue to provide transport since it was their delay that was holding up Henry's education. But when she rang the council to arrange the transport Wandsworth steadfastly refused to allow Henry to stay, with or without transport. They said he had a school to go to and that was Paddock. Angela argued that surely we could not be expected to send him to Paddock until the tribunal had reported its findings, but Wandsworth were implacable. Angela rang us close to tears – she couldn't believe the appalling pressure we were being put under. She was now too frightened to readmit Henry – she feared for her job. We understood, Angela was a good friend and we would never have wished to jeopardise her situation. But we were devastated. Our son was to be without a school.

Henry's education saga was fast becoming a full-time job. We wrote letters to as many influential people as possible, including Sir Michael Bichard, the then Permanent Secretary of State at the Department of Education. His reply was extremely compassionate – he promised to write to Wandsworth on our behalf, and he did. We also wrote to Bert Massie, Chairman of the Disability Rights Commission, and he too wrote on our behalf to ask Wandsworth if Henry could stay at Greenmead until the tribunal was resolved. Wandsworth dismissed both pleas. They knew they were untouchable.

Each discovery along the way came as yet another bitter blow. The next was the realisation that if we were to have any chance of winning at the tribunal we needed legal representation. The tribunal is supposed to be user-friendly and free. In fact it's a terrifying ordeal and anything but free – there are enormous costs involved. No wonder only 1 per cent of parents in our position actually go to tribunal. It's simply too costly and too daunting. Not only did we need lawyers, but the lawyers would need written reports from all the different therapists outlining Henry's needs. Michael and I were understandably depressed at the prospect of going to tribunal, and desperately wanted to avoid it.

To make matters worse, we had also been drawn into a battle for Freddie. We had discovered that he was not receiving any individual speech therapy, physiotherapy or occupational therapy at school. We had sent him to special needs school so that he could specifically receive these therapies to help his development. But because the therapy recommendations were only in the discretionary part of his statement, they didn't have to be delivered. To get them transferred to the statutory part of his statement we would have to go to – you guessed it – a tribunal.

This meant getting another set of expensive reports done. Each therapist's report for each boy cost an average of £800 to £1,000. This was money we didn't have. We were going to have to borrow it. Michael's earnings were decreasing as he had to devote more and more time to the preparation of the two cases. I was beginning to work late every night juggling the Foundation work with the tribunal preparation. By the end of each day we were both left shattered.

By now it was late June and Henry was due to leave school in July. The tribunal wouldn't be held until November. Henry would miss an entire term. I was beside myself with worry – how on earth was I going to manage? I couldn't understand how Wandsworth could be so cruel. Couldn't they see that I already had a hard enough time caring for two severely disabled children? Angela Laxton's warning a year earlier, when we had so enthusiastically campaigned to keep the school open, came back to haunt us with its painful accuracy.

I thought things couldn't get worse, but I shouldn't have tempted fate. Freddie came home from school one afternoon a few days later with a note saying that he hadn't managed to eat lunch at all – he couldn't swallow. Freddie had been having choking episodes over many years, but they had always cleared and they had reduced over the past year. But this time was different, and nothing would shift the blockage. Even liquid came straight back up.

Freddie was exhausted, and we decided that this 'block' might clear if he slept it off. Perhaps something stressful had happened at school and it would ease with a night's sleep. But by morning the blockage hadn't cleared and the only thing to do was to head for hospital.

At St George's Accident and Emergency we were ushered into a room to wait. Henry had been left at home with Julia, the au pair. Freddie was fast becoming dehydrated, as he hadn't been able to drink for nearly twenty-four hours. We waited and waited as the hours ticked by, Freddie sitting on my lap in silent fear. Occasionally he would say he was thirsty and we would try to give him sips of water in the hope that the blockage would clear, but it didn't and he was unable to swallow the water.

At three that afternoon we were finally seen. Their first reaction was that Freddie had swallowed a toy which had obstructed his throat. I wasn't so sure – he'd long since grown out of chewing toys. I explained that he'd had regular choking episodes in the past. They suggested Freddie should have a barium scan. He would have to drink a white liquid and have an X-ray which they hoped would show up the offending blockage. I pointed out that Freddie could not drink. The liquid went down all right, but hit the block and came straight back up. He couldn't even swallow his saliva and was becoming acutely distressed at having to spit the whole time to get rid of it, though by now he was so dehydrated that he had hardly any moisture left in him. But the mouthful of barium drink had been enough to coat his throat and they went ahead with the X-ray. Clearly visible just behind his breastbone was an apparent obstruction. We were told that he would need immediate surgery to remove it. Both Michael and I were shocked. I didn't want to see my baby suffer any more – surely he'd had his share? Why was this happening? Wasn't life hard enough?

Until that moment I felt I had responded pretty well to the challenge of having two disabled children. I hadn't allowed myself to be despondent, I had tried hard, stayed positive. I'd hung on to my visions and done my best for the boys. But now I felt spent. I wasn't sure I could face the challenges any more. My heart was filled with terror for Freddie, who was behaving in the most grown-up fashion, quietly doing as he was asked and staying calm. I had never seen my Freddie like this before. Perhaps he knew this had to be done, and I was deeply grateful. That night he was admitted to surgery.

The surgeon came to see us straight after operating. He explained that Freddie had no blockage in his throat and the diagnosis was not good. He told us that over the years, as a result of Freddie's diaphragmatic hernia and the surgery he had had in infancy, the valve between his stomach and his throat had remained open instead of shutting, as it normally does. This meant that the acid from his stomach had travelled up and burned away his throat, building up a mass of scar tissue which had steadily narrowed his throat. He also said that Freddie must have been in immense pain and that his throat was so badly damaged that they had performed a biopsy to test for cancer, which thankfully was not present. During the operation the surgeon had gently stretched the scar tissue in Freddie's throat, in order to expand the opening and allow him to swallow again, but he was unable to tell us how effective or long-lasting this might be.

I felt my legs could no longer bear my weight. Michael looked grey. I'd seen him this way before, when Freddie was first born and we thought we would lose him. We both knew that this diagnosis held untold dangers and uncertainties for Freddie. I had never really felt that Freddie was mine to keep – perhaps neither of us had. Now I wondered if the time was coming when we would have to let him go. In the hours after his birth we had stared death in the face, knowing we could lose him at any moment, and the fear of this had never left us.

Most people take life for granted – I certainly did before. But after so nearly losing him I viewed Freddie differently. It made him all the more precious, and I felt I could never take his life for granted. During the early years he caught every bug going, but he wouldn't just catch a mild dose like other children. Each time it would develop into major illness. I remember one horrible period which went on for a year or so when he was very small. Freddie's immune system was badly damaged, and when exposed to normal bacteria he didn't have the right mechanisms to fight off infection. He regularly caught a bug called cryptosporidium. This is usually associated with very unclean places, but Freddie could catch it in the cleanest of settings. It meant that all the blood vessels in his guts would burst and he'd poo blood, while his temperature swung up and down. Even now it's hard to think about the fear I felt. I remember sitting there with endless glasses of warm water and a syringe, gently squirting water into his mouth so that he wouldn't become dehydrated. The thought of having him on drips filled me with horror. I still hadn't got over the picture of him with endless wires sticking out of every available vein after he was born.

He would also catch coughs so badly that he'd be bringing up black blood, and on another occasion as I was feeding him one of his eyes began to fill with blood – all the vessels in the eye had burst and no one could say why. After each bout of childhood illness Freddie was so painfully thin that his clothes hung off him. He had no reserves of immunity or energy and we struggled to build him up, all the time dreading the next bug which might tax his weakened system to its limit. Now we were facing a new and frightening condition, one filled with uncertainty and fear and with no prognosis for his future.

After talking to the surgeon we were taken to see Freddie in the ward where he lay asleep, a small figure wrapped in blankets and with a drip emerging from under a large plaster on his hand. We knew he'd hate that – he had a thing about stickers, let alone plasters. At school they would give out stickers as rewards, but the moment Freddie got home he'd say, 'Off, off' in disgust and I had to rip it off. A little later he woke, with his throat unbearably sore. His bravery astounded both of us – there wasn't a single murmur or complaint. I promised to buy him whatever present he wanted. A few hours later we took him home.

Two weeks later Henry left school. I wept. My feelings of loss were enormous. The staff at Greenmead had been like family. It had been warm and cosy, and they had nurtured and cared for our precious son. Now he was being left out in the cold with nowhere to go.

We set off to spend the summer in Cornwall, still worried about the tribunals and in a deep state of shock over Freddie's condition. We had left hospital with no prognosis for his future and no advice or instructions on how to feed him. What we were soon to discover was that his throat was already tightening again. We had thought he would be able to eat normally, but soon even soft food was becoming harder for him to swallow.

A week later his throat blocked again, and nothing would shift the bolus of food jammed in his throat. We rang St George's to ask what to do. We were a six-hour drive away. They rang us back shortly afterwards to say that none of the hospitals en route to London could cope with the specialised surgery Freddie needed. Stretching his very restricted and delicate oesophagus required great surgical skill. We had no choice but to return.

It was a nightmarish drive to London with Freddie quietly choking for the entire drive. He had become withdrawn and his eyes looked depressed. He knew the pain he was about to endure. When we arrived at the hospital we were taken up to one of the children's wards and allocated a bed. We were told that the senior surgeon only worked here on Wednesdays and, as this was a Thursday, he was not available. The operation would be performed by a junior surgeon.

That evening Freddie, who had again gone without food and water for the entire day, was beginning to dehydrate. Not once did he complain, though occasionally he looked at me with sorrowful eyes. But when the time came for him to go into surgery he had hysterics at putting the horrid white gown on. I wished it was me instead – I would have done anything to lessen his pain.

Halfway through the operation the junior surgeon abandoned surgery as he feared he might have pierced Freddie's oesophagus. There was no choice but to wait and see whether our son was all right. I was given a rather uncomfortable pull-out chair next to Freddie's bed to sleep on. It didn't matter, though – I didn't sleep a wink that night. I lay there watching him and wondering if, after some future inevitable operation, the surgeons would come and tell me that my son had just died. I knew that from here on we would live in fear.

Thankfully, it turned out that the surgeon had not pierced Freddie's throat. But he hadn't managed to stretch it, either. Freddie would need a repeat operation before long. We drove home to Wandsworth in silence. My offer of the toy of his choice seemed far too small a recompense for how much he was suffering. Angela had generously rushed over to help with Henry, and when we arrived home she helped us settle both boys into bed. We collapsed on to the sofa, feeling numb and despondent, and turned on the television. Channel flicking, I came across a programme called *Phantoms of the Brain*. It was about a neuroscientist based in California, Professor Ramachandran. I couldn't believe it as I watched – his way of explaining the mechanics of the brain was like coming home. He talked of 'blind sight' – when the eye sees but the brain doesn't receive the message. This was a term that had been used about Henry more than ten years earlier.

I knew this was the man to contact, but I had no idea how. I typed his name into the Internet and up came his email address. I felt tremendously apprehensive – how would I get his attention? Probably the whole world was emailing him. I wrote four lines: 'I saw your programme. I have a son who is a mystery to the medical profession – he has no brain damage but can't walk or talk and has blind sight. Do you have any ideas?' A week later he replied. Would I send Henry's case history over? I had to obtain copies of all his notes. Every test had come back

NAD (nothing abnormal detected) so I guessed they wouldn't be much use, but I decided I would send them anyway. In what was fast turning out to be the year from hell, there was at last a faint ray of hope. Perhaps Professor Ramachandran would be able to help Henry.

Chapter 14

We had returned to Cornwall a few days after Freddie's second operation. For the rest of the summer he seemed to be managing well, though we had to watch him like hawks and keep him on a very restricted diet of soft, mushy foods. In September he was able to go back to school, but the fear was always there: we knew his throat could block at any moment. It wasn't just food that could cause his throat to restrict, stress could do it too, and our lives were becoming more stressful by the day.

I felt terribly afraid at the prospect of Henry having no school. How was I going to manage? The one blessing was that Professor Ramachandran was on board. I had immediately retrieved copies of Henry's notes from St George's and sent them to him. I asked him if he wanted Henry's old MRI scans – I knew they were out-of-date but they seemed fundamental to assessing Henry. Much to my surprise, he said no.

I had arranged for Henry to go to my mother's primary school for a couple of mornings a week with Julia, as I didn't want him to miss out on the company and sounds of other children. I was afraid he would become isolated and lonely. The head teacher was incredibly tolerant. He had already had Freddie in the class for several years and was now being asked to take Henry, who would be a twelve-year-old in a class of four-year-olds. The compassion he showed us was in stark contrast to our treatment by Wandsworth. Julia didn't drive, so we had to pay for taxis. This was going to rack up a big bill, but we felt we had to do it.

Next we asked Michael's mum, Lamorna, if she would have Henry two mornings a week. My two sisters-in-law offered to help look after him on those days, but we still had to drive Henry to Surrey and back each day – a round trip of two hours, which meant four hours' driving a day. This was going to make a huge dent in our working day, but we had to do it in order to get any work time at all. At one point, desperate for a few hours in which to work, I asked my sister Tilly to help me out with Henry for a couple of mornings. She agreed, but asked to be paid.

There were times when I couldn't help feeling resentful that we hadn't been offered more help by either of our families. I understood that there was no obligation on their part to help – they had their own lives and families to cope with. And they couldn't know just how desperate and exhausted we felt. None the less, we longed for someone to ring up and say, 'Bring the boys over. We'll have them for the weekend.'

We had eleven weeks to go until Henry's tribunal. The drive to Surrey was costly, time-consuming and exhausting, but we knew we'd just have to survive it for that time. Two weeks into this arduous routine Freddie got a blockage again and we headed back to the hospital for more surgery. Once again his poor agonised throat was stretched.

This time we were told that he needed major surgery, since it was doubtful whether stretching much more was feasible. Each time his throat shrank back, having lost the elasticity of normal unscarred tissue. The surgery would be performed at Great Ormond Street and would involve replacing his throat with his stomach. We would need a team of carers to help with Henry while we were away with Freddie in hospital. If we couldn't find such cover Freddie's surgery would have to wait, putting him in increasing danger. In desperation we rang our social worker, who agreed to write to Wandsworth education department imploring them to allow Henry back to Greenmead so that we could be with Freddie during his surgery. They refused.

Freddie's surgery had to be postponed. All we could do was pray that the latest operation to stretch his throat would give him more time. Meanwhile, desperate to help him, I started to trawl the Internet for alternatives.

Our immediate task, preparing all the documentation for the tribunal, was awesome. We met with endless therapists who each cost a fortune. Every day was dominated by appointments with lawyers and therapists or driving Henry to and from Surrey. The pressure on Michael and me was enormous. By evening we were exhausted and would collapse into a silent heap. We started to share a bottle of wine every evening, just to dull our senses and help us believe that this nightmare cycle would end and one day everything would be well.

The girls at the Foundation had no idea what we were going through. All they could see was that I had taken my eye off the ball and was not offering the support that, as their employer, I should. Our friends too could not relate to our current dilemmas. Our thoughts were filled with tribunals and surgery, and in company we probably became rather dull guests. When we talked about what was going on in our lives we could see the glaze in people's eyes. It was so far removed from their own lives that they couldn't relate to it, and after making a few sympathetic noises they wanted to move on. We felt that no one wanted to know, and that our position as the parents of disabled children set us apart from most other people and made us second-class citizens.

A parent of a child in mainstream education can pick the school of their choice, and if the school accepts the child then the place is secure. Not so in the disabled world – we had no right of choice. If the parent of a mainstream child fights for their child, the parent is applauded for trying hard on the child's behalf and their views are respected. As parents of disabled children we rapidly found that we were labelled hysterical and de-manding for fighting for our children's best interests, and our views were ignored and ridiculed. Imagine saying to the parent of a mainstream child that they must spend £20,000 to enable their child to access the national curriculum. Uproar, shock and horror would ensue. The headlines would read, 'Child Denied Maths, English, Sciences'. But there is no fanfare for the disabled child because in our society disabled children don't count. Discrimination is the norm.

It was now some weeks since I had sent Henry's notes to Professor Ramachandran, so I emailed him. Surely, I thought, he would have looked at them by now – he had seemed so enthusiastic and curious about Henry. After all, here was a boy who had no brain damage at all, yet who didn't function – it seemed perfectly natural to me that a top neuroscientist should be interested. I had never been able to understand why they hadn't been interested here in the UK.

When Ramachandran did reply he was rather vague and seemed to have forgotten our last email correspondence. Then he said he wanted us to organise new MRI scans. I replied that I had no contact with any hospital now. We were long out of the system, having been pretty well dumped after Henry's MRIs had come back normal nearly nine years earlier.

I knew Ramachandran had connections to Queen's Square, one of the largest neurological hospitals in London, so I asked him if he could refer us. He didn't reply. It was all rather frustrating – why, oh why, couldn't he keep up a dialogue? And why couldn't he look at Henry's old scans to start with? After all, it was still the same brain.

A couple of weeks later Michael had to go to New York for the Asian Art sales held by Christie's. I knew he felt guilty at leaving me to cope with the boys, and he assured me he'd get on an emergency flight if Freddie needed to go into hospital. It must have been a bit of a relief to get away from all the home battles, I wished I could have escaped too – I longed for a bit of respite.

Michael arrived in New York late on Monday evening and planned to view the sales the next morning. He rang me at about five o'clock on Tuesday afternoon, so excited he could hardly speak. There at the sales, standing right next to him, was Ramachandran. Michael had recognised him from the television programme and had introduced himself. Ramachandran was a collector of Indian art and was delighted to meet Michael. They went off to have coffee together to discuss Indian art and Henry's brain.

Neither of us could believe the coincidence. I felt a wave of hope and optimism. Ramachandran had promised Michael he'd come to England to see Henry and organise the scans. I felt I could survive anything if Henry was to receive help at last.

Now, with renewed energy and some of our faith in life restored, we decided to put all we had into winning against Wandsworth. We felt so angry that we had to face a tribunal that I decided to do all I could to highlight the way we were being treated. I asked Alastair Stewart if he could get a letter to Margaret Hodge, the then Parliamentary Under Secretary of State in the Department of Education and Employment. In it I told her about our case and asked if she could help. I had enough evidence to prove that all was not well regarding Henry's transition, and I knew she had the power to intervene.

Alastair was very into politics, and I knew he would get my letter to her desk if he could. He agreed, and duly delivered it. Her response, I guess, was what I expected. She couldn't intervene in an isolated case. OK, I thought, I'll find ten families. Once in the stranglehold of the tribunal system, we had met many other distraught families, all fighting for the right school environment for their children. The sheer numbers horrified me, and the huge amount of money that these parents, like us, were being forced to spend was an outrage – let alone the waste of taxpayers' money spent on unnecessary tribunals.

Local education authorities were forcing parents into fighting for their children's rights and the whole thing was a scandal. The LEAs did not have to pay for the tribunals; that money came from a separate budget. So they could force as many parents as they liked to take them to tribunals without any loss to themselves. And of course most parents couldn't begin to find the money and energy to fight the system on top of caring for a disabled child, so 99 per cent of them had to accept whatever bizarre, cruel or unjust option their LEA had chosen for their child. But of those parents who did make it to tribunals, over 90 per cent won their cases.

I produced ten families for Margaret Hodge and she ignored me. I battered on door after door after door. I asked Felicity Kendal if she knew the Prime Minister. She said she knew Cherie as they shared a hairdresser. I asked if she'd get a letter to Cherie. I was sure that as a mother of four she would be interested, especially as she was into human rights and I felt our human rights were being breached. After all, we'd had a gun held to our heads: 'If you want education for your children you'll have to fight for it – that's the price you must pay.' Felicity gave Cherie the letter, in which I told her about our case and the piles of other families' testimonials, all relaying the same awful injustice, but Cherie's secretary wrote back to say that she could not intervene unless I did it through a solicitor – at vast cost. I felt miffed. I had hoped she would remember my name. A year earlier she had borrowed an Indian necklace from Michael at Spink and Son, and in return she had promised to make a donation to the Henry Spink Foundation. No donation ever came the Foundation's way, and now there was not even a flicker of interest in our case.

But I wasn't about to give up – who else could I try? Who would be troublesome to the government? Who liked an underdog? Of course! Ken Livingstone – but how to reach him? I called Alastair Stewart again and he generously promised personally to forward a letter to Ken and make sure he got it. Alastair was a great ally and appeared to be one of the few people to see what was truly going on. He recommended I keep a diary of events, as it was fast becoming highly entertaining material. I told him I'd been keeping an audio diary since Freddie was born. It had been therapeutic, but I also wanted to record the highs and lows as they came. I knew that if I ever wrote a book my memory would edit the past unless I had recorded it in all its gory detail, including the fact that you could want to die one day and the next see a miracle unfold.

After writing my letter it dawned on me that if Ken agreed to a meeting I should try to set up a photo shoot. The only name I could think of was Max Clifford, a publicist famous for being behind many major 'kiss and tell' exposés. I wasn't sure he'd be the right person to go to, or even interested, but it was worth a go. At the same time I had contacted the *Express* newspaper and had been put in touch with Jane Warren, a senior feature writer. I'd explained our story and she had agreed to write a piece. I mentioned Max, and she thought he might help as he had a disabled daughter himself.

I felt very nervous contacting Max out of the blue. But what the hell – I had nothing to lose and I wanted a photo shoot with Ken. Then someone might just take note of what was happening to disabled children in our country. It was worth a try.

So I rang Max, who was charming and invited me round to his office. He had bright blue eyes that stared right through you without blinking. I could see him assess me in seconds – was I worth bothering with? Luckily for me he decided I was. He asked his daughter Louise, who worked with him, if she would help organise the publicity.

Max was a sharp and clever operator, and he was also enormously generous. On that first visit he and Louise offered Henry and Freddie the use of their hyperbaric oxygen therapy tank, given to them by a rich client in Canada. The tank simulated the effect of deep sea diving, and the theory was that the pressurised oxygen would help to alleviate disorders such as cerebral palsy and the vicious and crippling form of arthritis from which Louise suffered. This instant generosity was totally unexpected and lovely. They were happy for us to come over and invade their private home with Henry and Freddie, and I thought it incredibly kind. I didn't take them up on it simply because I was afraid the tank would frighten the boys.

Ken Livingstone agreed to meet us. He was a fascinating man and the moment he met us he put us at our ease. His skill was such that we instantly felt we'd known him for years. He was charming, funny, a great raconteur and quick to wing my message into the publicity machine.

The London *Standard* ran a piece. Our local papers ran the saga almost weekly. The *News of the World* covered it and so did ITV and Radio 4's *You and Yours*. None of it made a blind bit of difference.

I found it hard to believe that ministers could sleep at night. Were they ignorant or did they just not care? Nothing I did, even with an ever-growing list of families, could penetrate the government's ruthlessly hard heart. We had no choice but to go to tribunal.

As the date drew nearer we both felt our nerves were stretched to snapping point. We were thoroughly exhausted from driving Henry miles for a few hours' care to enable us to work. And the poor boy himself was beginning to look depressed. The monotony and relentlessness of it was taking its toll on everyone. On top of which we were both becoming concerned about money, since we had such high outgoings and very little to sustain them. Michael was simply unable to put in the hours to earn enough. We couldn't go on much longer this way.

The day of the tribunal is one I shall never forget. I hardly slept a wink the night before. My child's future was in the hands of a bunch of people who had never even met him. I caught sight of myself in the mirror just before we left. I wondered who this strained, exhausted woman staring back at me was. What had become of me? I felt nauseous and was shaking. Another parent who had already been through a tribunal had suggested I should take beta-blockers; they had helped him and his wife through their ordeal. I had said no but now wished I hadn't been quite so brave – I wanted to be sick. Michael and I sat in stony silence as the taxi ground its way through the heavy rush-hour traffic.

We arrived in Victoria Street in Central London and found the tribunal building. As we passed through the revolving doors I wondered how many other traumatised parents had pushed their way in here as part of their journey to hell and back on behalf of their beloved children. I felt every nerve ending screaming in anticipation of the ordeal ahead. My adrenaline was running on red alert. After registering our names at the reception desk we were directed to a private waiting room attached to our tribunal room.

Our barrister arrived and explained that we couldn't win on the expenses argument. There would be no dispute: the law clearly stated that a parent could not choose an out-of-borough school if it was over £1,000 a year more expensive than the in-borough school. Our choice was £4,000 more expensive. We would have to prove that Paddock, the LEA's choice, could not meet Henry's needs.

The day passed in a blur. I soon realised that we were up against a machine that was unstoppable. Wandsworth was in full swing, giving evidence that left us both reeling. Bedelsford could offer Henry speech therapy, physiotherapy, sensory gardens, swimming, soft play rooms and sensory rooms all on site. Paddock had none of these facilities, but Wandsworth was claiming it had them all. Michael and I couldn't believe what was happening. When Michael gave evidence he said, 'We know you don't have these facilities at Paddock – we have a child already at the school.' The day went from bad to worse, our spirits rapidly sinking. We already had the cost arguments against us. Would the tribunal panel believe us rather than Wandsworth about the non-existent facilities?

I was later to discover that, even though the tribunal is an arm of the High Court, the evidence given there is not under oath. Local education authorities can knowingly go to a tribunal and lie. We'd had no idea what we were up against. By the time we left we had spent nine hours closeted in this stuffy room listening to evidence and arguments, with only a brief break.

We returned home half-dead with shock and exhaustion. As we walked through the door we could clearly see Freddie standing in the kitchen with a major choking episode in full flow. We gathered him up and headed for St George's. I wondered if God had finally decided to abandon us.

Chapter 15

The next two weeks were as close to hell as I ever want to go. We were waiting for the tribunal verdict and I had both boys out of school. Freddie was recovering from his latest bout of surgery and Henry was totally demoralised and depressed by his limited environment. All I could do was to pray that we would win – I needed Henry back in school.

One Saturday morning I was lying in the bath, enjoying a quiet moment while both boys were still asleep. The post arrived and I heard Michael go down to collect it. I could hear him tearing open an envelope and then the slow, heavy tread of his step as he climbed the stairs towards the bathroom. He looked ashen. We had lost, he told me. The tribunal had ruled against us and Henry was to go to Paddock.

I felt devastated. Paddock was the wrong school for Henry in every way. At that moment I felt I had lost my faith in God and humanity. I had even lost my faith in hoping. Michael and I crumpled. We didn't bother to read the whole of the tribunal decision – all we could see was the end result. That weekend was one of the hardest I can remember. Every ounce of fight left us. I wished someone would step in and take the children off our hands – we needed to grieve for a few hours. But there was no one, and we had to try to stay strong for the boys.

On the Monday our solicitor phoned and said we could appeal. I could hardly take in what he was saying. I'd run out of hope and now here was hope again. He said the tribunal panel's response was written in such a way as almost to invite an appeal.

But while this news was truly welcome, we still faced enormous problems. The appeal would take several months – even if we were successful Henry wouldn't be at school until well into the next year. He was getting so depressed that I was really worried about him. Why wouldn't Wandsworth let him stay at his old school until this was resolved? Why punish Henry?

On closer inspection of the tribunal decision we discovered that they had awarded Henry all the therapies he would have had on-site at Bedelsford. This gave us grounds to appeal. Paddock could not provide the therapies and therefore they would have to be bought in, turning the situation around and making Paddock an 'inefficient use of resources'. The problem was that it was up to us to prove that Paddock didn't have the in-house facilities Wandsworth were claiming it had. We had seven days to gather evidence and enter our appeal.

For a parent to be able to approach the tribunal system on a level playing field you need to be a trained lawyer and accountant with six months to spare to gather all the evidence you need. Add to this endless stamina and persistence, and you might just stand a chance. Our position felt pretty hopeless. What could we do that we hadn't already done? I felt like giving up.

Then something snapped inside me. Here I was, looking after two disabled children, running a charity without
pay, I'd had Freddie in hospital six times in six months
and Henry excluded from school . . . but by God I was
damned if Wandsworth were going to beat me. They'd
picked the wrong family to bully. We weren't going to go
away. We would fight on and do whatever it took to win.
Apart from anything else, I felt I couldn't let down the
other families who were fighting too. I set to with an
extraordinary new-found energy.

What could we do, I wondered, to make a difference
this time? After all, I had already tried drumming up
publicity and writing to politicians and people in authority, with no success at all. I don't know whether they felt
they could safely bracket me in the same basket as my
disabled children, but they sure as hell were not interested in what was going on. That meant there was
nothing for us to do but find fresh evidence and make
sure it was strong enough for us to win.

Michael's work had been deeply affected by this continuous struggle – I was desperately worried about how we
were going to manage. So far it had cost us about half a
year's salary in missed work and £20,000 in professional
and legal fees – money we would have to borrow. I was
also still desperately trying to run the charity, but it was
beginning to look as though the five years' hard work I'd
put into getting it off the ground and making it a success
were going to go down the drain. The Foundation had lost
around £80,000 through my lack of fundraising and I had
no idea how I was going to catch up or keep it afloat. I just
prayed that we could keep going until all this was over.

I knew there were lessons to be learned. Finding out that we could appeal had given me back some hope. I believe that everything has a message and I felt sure that something positive would come out of this. Just what that was, though, I had no idea. Peter, the medium, helped me to get through this incredibly tough time and gave me the courage to keep battling for the boys. He told me that we would win in the end and that I would become involved in getting the laws for disabled children changed. But even with his support it was sometimes hard to imagine how I would keep going or to believe that we might win.

We had no idea what our next move was until a parent at my mother's school, Gavin Millar, heard of our plight and offered to help. He was a QC and he agreed to take on our appeal for free. I hardly dared hope that the tide might be turning in our favour. The tribunal agreed that we could appeal against their first ruling provided, as our solicitor had told us, we gathered evidence to prove our case. They listed what they wanted, in particular evidence relating to the supposed sensory garden at Paddock.

We frantically set about preparing our case. There wasn't a minute to lose. We had to get a copy of Wandsworth's Special Educational Needs (SEN) department's budget sheets relating to the costs at Paddock. A friend, Celia, had gone through a similar ordeal several years earlier and she knew where to get copies of the accounts. Together we set off for our local library. We headed for the reference section, where the accounts would be kept. I asked the girl if she could dig them out. She turned to a row of boxes on a shelf and sifted through them. They were missing. I asked her if it was a large document, to which she said no. I then asked if it would be possible for her to telephone Wandsworth and ask them to fax the figures across. After all, they were on public record and should have been in the library.

She disappeared into a back room and after a few minutes popped her head round the door and said she was sorry but she wouldn't be able to get the figures for us.

I refused to be defeated. We went to another library – the accounts we wanted weren't there either. Another parent tried his local library for me, also with no success. There were no copies to be had.

When we got home I decided to try to obtain the cost of transporting the boys to the school, the next item on my list of evidence. Wandsworth had claimed that it would cost £33,000 a year to take Henry to school because he wouldn't fit on the existing bus and would need special transport just for him. I rang the transport company which supplied Wandsworth to try to confirm this and check the cost, but they wouldn't speak to me. I was blocked.

By this time I was in such turmoil I hardly knew which way to turn. I couldn't believe the lengths to which the SEN department were prepared to go to cover their tracks. I felt as if I was stepping into the pages of a spy novel.

Michael rang the Department of Education and asked if they could send us the accounts. They explained that we had to get the figures from Wandsworth. I rang the

Wandsworth accounts department. The official I spoke to gave me a set of figures which didn't tally with the figures presented by the SEN department at the tribunal. I rang back and he gave me a completely different set of figures and then refused to speak to me any further.

I rang our solicitor and said we were being blocked at every avenue. Our solicitor sent a letter over to Wandsworth saying that he would write to the tribunal president asking for a letter of disclosure to be sent out. Wandsworth didn't cooperate so that's exactly what happened. We then received a letter banning us from contacting Wandsworth council other than through a solicitor. We couldn't believe it was legal to ban us – we decided it was just another power game to stop us gathering evidence. They were playing for time – a luxury we didn't have. We had only a few days left to gather our evidence.

We tried a new tactic. Michael set off for Paddock with a camera to take photographs of the non-existent sensory garden that Wandsworth had claimed the school had. When he got there the head teacher seemed flustered, but she allowed Michael to take the photos. The next day, after dropping Henry off at his mother's, Michael was passing Wandsworth town hall on the way home when he rang me on his mobile to say he was going straight in to collect the figures. He had a right to them and would not be barred.

At first they refused to hand them over. Michael wouldn't give them his name, but he knew they knew who he was. He refused to leave until they handed the figures over.

He got them.

By the time he got home he was shaking from the exertion of it all. I took one look at page after page after page of endless, meaningless numbers and wept – I had no idea how even to begin to interpret the figures. Michael, though, was undaunted. He calmly spent several hours working it all out. We drew a blank over the annotations B1 to B5 next to all the figures. Michael telephoned the Department of Education and they explained that disabled kids were banded between 1 and 5, depending on the categorisation of their disability. Globally Developmentally Delayed children such as Henry were Band 1 – the most expensive.

Wandsworth had said, both to us and to the tribunal, that Paddock cost £10,026. But that figure was the average cost per child, and the banding system altered it completely. As a Band 1 child Henry would in fact cost £12,534. The gap between the cost of the two schools was closing. Now all we had to do was add on the cost of the therapies that Wandsworth would have to buy in for Henry and we could prove that it would in fact be far cheaper to send him to Bedelsford. We spent a hellish few days researching the cost of various professionals' services, ringing up physiotherapists and speech therapists and putting together a detailed cost analysis. We estimated that to buy in the therapies would cost Wandsworth £28,000 a year.

Next we tackled Wandsworth's claim that it would cost them £33,000 to transport Henry to Bedelsford. When I told Bert Massie, Chairman of the Disability Rights Commission, he roared with laughter, said he hoped it was a Rolls Royce they were going to use and recommended I apply for the job as driver as it would be a nice little earner! Sue, Albert's mum, measured the bus the other children went on and told me that another wheelchair could fit into it perfectly well. She agreed to come to the appeal as a witness.

By the time the week was up we believed we had proof that Paddock was actually the more expensive option. We submitted our evidence and prayed. The appeal was allowed, and was set for 6 February 2001.

But before that date, just a couple of weeks later we were back in Victoria Street for Freddie's tribunal, attempting to win him the therapy which had been recommended in his statement. Freddie's case illustrated the madness of the system very well. One of the witnesses Wandsworth put forward was the educational psychologist who had assessed Freddie in the first place and said he needed maximum therapy input. I wondered what she would say – she could hardly undo what she had recommended. And guess what, on the day of the tribunal she was replaced with a new recruit eager to please Wandsworth and very happy to thwart us.

We had been warned that some panels were on the side of the parents and others not. This panel didn't like us; its members looked bored. In the end we managed to obtain fifteen minutes of speech therapy for Freddie each week. Nine hours a year. These nine hours would cost the education department £450 per year. Their barrister cost £1,500 to contest the therapy, and the day at the tribunal cost the taxpayer £20,000.

We spent that Christmas in Cornwall. Julia was on

holiday and we couldn't afford any other care, so the two of us had to manage. We were both at dropping point. Not long before Christmas I'd gone to Biolab to pick up some supplements for the boys and had bumped into our old friend Dr John Maclaren Howard. When he saw me he stepped back with a look of concern on his face and told me I looked awful. I'd laughed and told him that we were being put through the mill over the boys' education, that Henry was without a school and that I was exhausted.

John had taken me into his office, wired me up to a monitor and asked me a string of questions. It took him twenty minutes to diagnose that I had a leaking heart valve. He said it was no wonder that I felt awful and that I must rest. I mentioned this later to our social worker, who said that if I could prove I was dying I might get some extra help.

We returned to London in early January 2001, praying that the appeal would result in a school place for Henry and ease a little of our load. We were even more worried now about Freddie. He could only eat very soft food, and even so every meal was terrifying. We knew that his throat could block again at any time and that he really couldn't take much, if any, more throat-stretching surgery. His doctors still wanted to perform the major surgery which involved replacing his throat with his stomach and had booked him in for the operation, but we were very concerned about how drastic it seemed.

I'd been trawling the Internet in a desperate attempt to find help for him and had come across a wonderful site in America offering advice to sufferers of GORD – gastro oesophageal reflux disorder. When I contacted them a lovely, friendly woman called Beth had responded. I explained Freddie's problem and told her about the major surgery the hospital was suggesting.

Beth told me that if we proceeded with this operation – which, as far as she was concerned, had gone out with the ark in the USA – Freddie could be left in a far worse condition. In the States the procedure had been replaced by keyhole surgery. Most reflux sufferers have poor swallowing action, and major surgery with no prior testing could result in no swallowing action at all. It was vital, she urged, to have some motility tests done on Freddie to check his swallowing. No one here had mentioned these tests to us. Beth also asked me if we'd tried motility drugs as an interim measure. These were drugs that could aid swallowing and stop the strictures occurring with such ease. We'd never heard of these, either.

After learning this I wanted to speak to the surgeon before we admitted Freddie. Michael rang St George's where a rather surly girl answered the phone. No, we were told, the surgeon's diary was full and he couldn't fit us in – goodbye. We knew the surgeon practised at a private hospital nearby, so we decided our best bet was to go privately – it would be our only chance of seeing him. We rang reception and asked to speak with his secretary. She said his private secretary was based at St George's but the number she gave us was different from the one Michael had dialled for the NHS appointment.

Michael duly rang and the same girl answered the phone, now speaking in a very pleasant voice. Yes, of course we could make an appointment to see the surgeon. What time would we like? She suggested that we ask for a reduction as she 'knew' that he couldn't see us on the NHS schedule. We couldn't stop laughing.

The surgeon looked mortified when he realised what had happened, and didn't charge us for the appointment. He also put Freddie straight on motility drugs – 'Isn't he on them already'? I wanted to thump him. These drugs would alter Freddie's life, and no one had even mentioned them to us. A small advisory website somewhere in the USA had probably saved my child's life. I thanked God and I thanked Beth.

Soon the day of the appeal arrived. This was our third trip to Victoria Street and it wasn't getting any easier. My resentment at being put through a farce by a bunch of budget-crazed bureaucrats was beginning to get to me. I couldn't face sitting opposite the head teacher of Paddock or the SEN team. I glared at them as hard as I could.

I didn't realise until we got to the tribunal that so far we had only been invited to appeal, and therefore before it could go ahead we still had to win the right to appeal. Wandsworth were plainly banking on us not winning the right to appeal – in which case no evidence would be heard and nothing would change. This is why they hadn't backed down, despite the evidence they knew we now had.

I could see the chair of the panel trying to catch my eye with a sympathetic look. I dared not interpret it to our advantage – though I could see she was trying to encourage me. We'd had our hopes raised before, only to have them cruelly dashed. I remained terrified.

Gavin, our QC, and Wandsworth's barrister had to

battle it out between them to get the tribunal to decide whether we could or could not appeal. It took four hours of debating before we took a lunch break while the panel made their decision. When we reconvened my heart was racing. The chair announced that we had won our right to appeal. *Yes*!

Now came the actual appeal. We went through all the points. Henry could fit on the existing bus and we were able to prove it. Paddock didn't have any of the facilities or therapies that they had claimed they had – we even had the photographs to prove there was no sensory garden.

By now it was five o'clock and we were numb with exhaustion. The last of the criteria to be discussed were the actual costs of the schools. We already knew they had misquoted the true cost of sending Henry to Paddock. But now I sat listening in disbelief as the true cost of *both* schools emerged. Our QC looked bemused, the panel looked blank and Michael and I froze.

The sole reason that our lives had been turned upside down was the comparative costs of the two schools. Our choice of school had apparently been £4,154 more expensive than the council's option. Yet now Wandsworth was saying that Kingston, where Bedelsford was, had made a mistake. The cost of Bedelsford was in fact £9,646. Paddock cost £12,534 for Henry, as we knew from the figures we had obtained. In other words this was a total reversal in the figures – the case should never have gone to tribunal in the first place.

We felt certain that no one had made a mistake. Wandsworth knew exactly how much Bedelsford cost

– they had children there already. We'd had the right to choose Bedelsford from the start. All the agony and expense had been for nothing. We spent the next two weeks in an exhausted, stunned limbo waiting for the tribunal panel's response.

It was a Tuesday morning. I was recording my audio diary: 'Michael has just telephoned me . . . we've won.' I switched off the tape, unable to speak. I just sat there crying, feeling a surge of relief but also a wave of deep exhaustion. I couldn't stop the tears – I went on and on weeping.

I wanted to speak to my mother. I rang her but I couldn't speak – the poor receptionist at her school could hardly get my name out of me. My mother immediately assumed, as I choked with sobs, that we'd lost, but eventually I managed to get out the words to tell her that we'd won. The panel had ordered that we be informed by phone, without waiting for their decision in writing, and Michael had taken the call at work. He told me he'd rung back after half an hour to ask them to repeat it.

Henry started at Bedelsford after the spring half-term.

Chapter 16

Sending Henry back to school was harder than I expected. He had been at home for five months and, much as I longed to see him happy in school, I was anxious about how he would make the transition. He'd been depressed for the last couple of months – would he be able to cope with a brand-new school? In fact he took to it immediately and was thrilled to be back with other children, leaving me to mop up my anxious mother's tears and get back to work.

This wasn't easy. The strain of having Henry without a school and Freddie in surgery so many times had been enormous, and picking up the pieces of our lives afterwards was going to take time and effort. Added to which, Wandsworth were still not treating us nicely. Henry was to be collected first on the bus every morning, which would involve a pick-up time of 7 a.m. This meant we had to get up at 5.30, as it took the two of us that long to get both boys ready for school. It also meant that Henry was on the bus for a total of four hours a day getting to a school which was twenty minutes away. The two-hour journey to and from school would break Wandsworth's own travel guidelines of no more than one hour's travel either way to school – but we were fast learning that for local education authorities breaking rules meant nothing. No one cared and no one monitored what was going on.

Michael and I felt the result of the tribunal was a completely hollow victory. Bedelsford had been cheaper all along. The ordeal we had been put through had been unnecessary and should never have happened. How could a system allow such treatment of us with no retribution whatsoever? The past year had nearly destroyed our lives, yet Wandsworth could do this to anyone they chose without fear of penalty. Our income had plunged, the charity was short of funds – at a time when the forthcoming poster campaign would lead to many more calls for help – and both Michael and I were suffering from post-traumatic shock, though we didn't realise it at the time. It was another two years before we really began to get over the pain caused by it all.

Our anger at the injustice done to us was enormous. We couldn't believe that Wandsworth could get away with blithely saying, 'Kingston (the neighbouring borough) made an error' as an excuse for our ordeal and get away with it. We felt that those who had made the decisions shouldn't have been in office. We set about finding out whether we could get back the money we'd been forced to spend on the tribunal. It seemed reasonable to us that if we had been forced to tribunal on false grounds we should be compensated. In fact we were rather surprised that some kind of compensation hadn't been offered already.

During the tribunal we'd heard about a body called the Local Government Ombudsman. The tribunal literature clearly stated that if LEA maladministration had occurred while at tribunal, we could complain to the

Ombudsman. Good, we thought – we wanted an apology and our money back. We spent days compiling an outline of the case and highlighting the fact that, if the true costs of the schools had been made apparent before the start of the tribunal, it would never have been held. We felt our case was a very clear-cut one of maladministration and began to feel hopeful. We sent our bundle of papers off to the Ombudsman and waited.

A month later we received a reply stating that once we had been to tribunal we had no right to complain to the Ombudsman. We were amazed. We thought it clearly stated in the tribunal literature that we could. What the hell was going on?

A couple of years earlier, in the middle of preparations for one of our parties at St James's Palace, a man had wandered through to look for something in Prince Charles's office. He'd stopped and looked at one of our posters and had come over to me. I was busy putting bottles of champagne into ice buckets and didn't really have time to stop and chat, but none the less I did. I discovered that his name was David Baldwin and he was Sergeant of the Vestry at the Palace. He was a lovely man, and explained that he had a special needs son who suffered from autism. He and his wife had fought tooth and nail with Westminster LEA to secure appropriate education for their son and had eventually won their choice of school, but not until after they had been totally traumatised by the affair.

David had stayed in touch with us after that and was a great source of encouragement and advice during our education battles. So when we received the letter of refusal from the Ombudsman we turned to him for advice. He now told us that his father, Sir Peter Baldwin, had by amazing coincidence written the original Parliamentary Ombudsman legislation back in the 1960s. I went to see Sir Peter, now in his eighties, and asked him how the Ombudsman could reject our case. Had he meant the Ombudsman to refuse cases of maladministration after tribunal? He said categorically that the Ombudsman was misinterpreting the law and should be investigating our case.

We wrote again to the Ombudsman and were still refused. We turned to our lawyer, who told us that we could challenge the Ombudsman through a Judicial Review in the High Court but that it would cost us about £10,000. This was money we didn't have.

So, since this avenue was effectively blocked, I decided I would try to highlight the legal problem by writing to ministers and politicians. Surely someone would want to do something about this misinterpretation of the law.

Then one evening we received an unexpected phone call from Councillor Grimston, the elected Wandsworth member responsible for education, whose nickname, rather appropriately, was 'Grim'. He asked us for a meeting to discuss our children's needs. Michael, who took the call, nearly fell over backwards. We had spent an entire year telling Councillor Grimston what was going on and how we were being treated, and he had steadfastly ignored us. I knew that other families had also sought his help and been ignored.

Michael, rather bemusedly, agreed that he could come round to see us. Angela, Henry's old head teacher, advised us to feed him. He liked biscuits. I filled a bowl and awaited his arrival at eight that evening.

When he arrived, Grim, who was a large chap, seated himself on the sofa and stared mournfully at the bowl of biscuits carefully placed in front of him, but did not take a single one. He looked uncomfortable as we repeated our tale. We knew he'd seen our letter to the Ombudsman and were sure that was why he was here. Wandsworth were clearly as yet unaware that the Ombudsman would not investigate our case. When we'd finished Grim looked puzzled and behaved as though he had never heard any of the story before. He told us that none of it added up to him. Why put a family through hell if the parents' choice was cheaper from the start? It seemed crazy. Our point exactly, we said.

Gavin Millar, our QC, had a theory about what had happened. He thought it was to do with setting a precedent and trying to stop other kids from going to school out of borough. Every disabled child is granted a central government allowance of a few thousand pounds – it's called an SSA Allowance and it goes to the borough in which the child is at school. Henry's allowance would now go to Kingston, not Wandsworth. This money was not earmarked for special educational needs and could be spent elsewhere. Gavin's theory was that Wandsworth wanted to keep all the kids in borough, collect all the allowances and then siphon the money off to spend on exciting things like mending pavements which were far more vote-grabbing than disabled children.

I have no idea if Gavin's theory was right or not. Personally it was easy to imagine that Wandsworth had put us through hell for the sheer pleasure of it. The other families suffering at their hands all felt the same.

Either way, Grim kept muttering, 'Why should they have done it?' It clearly didn't make sense to him either. With his next breath he asked if we'd like to transfer Freddie to Bedelsford as he had outgrown Paddock. He offered us a taxi to take both boys to school. Lastly, he offered Henry the full thirty hours, one-to-one support he needed in school, instead of the ten hours gained at tribunal.

Why this sudden change of position? We had no idea and we didn't care. We gulped down our astonishment and accepted. But we also made it plain that we would fight on to change the system.

As a result of what we had been through we knew exactly what was needed to close the gaps in the law. The Ombudsman legislation that was blighting the lives of vulnerable children and their families must be rewritten to close the loophole and make LEAs accountable for their actions. The only problem was that no one in power wanted to know. I decided to put together a legal challenge. I knew so many miserable families all going through the same nightmarish unjust process that I just had to do something. I hadn't a clue how to do it, but I knew that getting the law changed was going to be my only way forward.

But for now Henry was settled and happy in his new school, and I was thrilled. And Freddie's throat seemed to be under control. I'd pretty much worked out what he could and couldn't eat and the medication was definitely helping; so we'd been able to cancel the surgery, which in any case we weren't at all sure about.

We'd also got a lovely new part-time carer, Sharon, who came for two hours after school every afternoon. Julia had left at around the time Henry started back at school and I'd dreaded the search for someone new until, by a stroke of luck, I'd found an agency called Special People which supplied staff to work with special needs children. Sharon had come from them and she was a delight, cheerful and capable. She was also willing to stay for a year. Could life at last be beginning to settle down?

Michael was due to attend the Asian Art fair in New York and I decided to go too. I hadn't had a day off in over a year and we'd had no time together at all and really needed some. We'd only be gone five days, and the thought of going away filled me with such relief that I hardly knew where to put myself.

I hadn't had much luck with Ramachandran in the year since he and Michael had met at the last fair. He didn't appear to have read Henry's medical notes and still hadn't come to London to see us or organised new MRI scans for Henry. It was all becoming mightily frustrating.

We were due to leave on the Tuesday morning and arrive in New York early that afternoon. Michael had fixed up a string of business appointments and I was set on a bit of retail therapy. Bliss. Angela and my mother would look after the boys either side of school. I had cooked and frozen all the boys' food for the week and had packed my suitcase. I was ready to go.

Just before we left I decided to pick up my emails. The first was from Ramachandran. His long-promised visit to meet Henry was going to happen at last. He would arrive in London several hours after our flight departed. I felt torn. I'd been emailing him about Henry for well over a year now and got nowhere. Now suddenly he was announcing his visit. I'm afraid it didn't take too long for me to decide which option I was going to go for. I needed time out. 'Don't worry,' he emailed. 'I'll see you in New York at the Asian Art fair.' He planned to fly from London to New York a day later. But he didn't leave me any contact details or respond to my next email asking for them, so we left for New York without much hope of making contact.

The opening night of the fair was to be a lavish affair. At least five thousand people would attend the event, all dressed up in their finery and hoping to be noticed. Michael went every year as he vetted the objects on sale, so he knew just about everyone. That evening we were on the stand, or 'booth' as the Americans call them, of a good friend of ours. Suddenly Ramachandran appeared out of nowhere. Of course he didn't know me, but I recognised him instantly. I gushed and he oozed charm. He promised to organise scans and he promised to come to London in the very near future to meet Henry. I felt happy but not convinced – by now I had begun to doubt his promises. But we did return to London feeling completely refreshed; it had been fantastic to have a few days' break.

The point had now come where we felt desperate enough to try social services again. Our file had already been closed twice, once after we failed to take up the eight hours a year of help with the laundry and again when Henry and Freddie were about four and eight. We had been at two disabled brothers' birthday party, boys from Henry's school. The carers looking after these two boys instantly asked us why we had no help and offered to come and do an assessment, as they were an independent agency sending carers to Wandsworth. We readily agreed to the assessment. When it was sent to Wandsworth they refused. No one ever told you what you were entitled to, and we just assumed we weren't entitled to anything.

But, now that the boys were growing older and bigger, they were getting harder to manage and we were becoming increasingly desperate for additional help. Although Sharon was excellent her hours were limited, and one part-time helper simply wasn't enough. It wasn't just a question of being desperate for a break or to have an hour's respite from the endless cycle of drudgery, it was the physical reality that I couldn't cope alone any longer. Henry needed two people to look after him. Bathing a five-foot-six teenager who's fitting and desperately trying to keep his head above water while his body goes rigid is terrifying. And while I would be struggling with Henry in the bath Freddie would be on the rampage through the house, a whirlwind of destructive activity emptying drawers and filing cabinets, switching on the gas and opening the front door if I'd forgotten to lock it. In my tape diary I recorded the details of a typical day in our lives. It gives a flavour of our desperation and exhaustion:

I wake at 2.30 a.m. to change Henry's nappy and just can't get back to sleep. By 4.30 a.m. I finally manage to nod off. The alarm clock peals at 5.30. My eyes yearn to stay closed but I force myself out of bed – our schedule is tight as the bus comes at 7 a.m. to pick Henry up. Freddie's comes half an hour later. It takes both of us an hour and a half to get the boys ready for school.

I rush down to prepare breakfast. It isn't just a question of pouring out the cereal and a quick drink of milk. There are endless supplements and medication to prepare for each child. I've got my time down to fifteen minutes on this task. Then it's back upstairs, where Michael is getting Freddie dressed. I finish him off and take him downstairs and start his breakfast. He has all his medication at the start so that we don't miss any out. I send in emergency medication to the school just in case one of us does forget something in the rush. He suffers terribly if the antacids are not given.

Michael gets Henry dressed and brings him downstairs. Either I feed Henry or Michael does. Henry's not easy to feed. Most meals take an hour – that's three hours a day just shovelling food. No wonder he doesn't like meals – he's probably as bored as we are. He has an amazing habit of flicking the spoon out of your hand just as you get it to his mouth and the cereal flies everywhere. Ideally it takes two people to feed Henry, one to hold his hands, but we can't afford that luxury most days.

While one of us struggles to feed Henry, the other takes Freddie to the loo and puts on a pull-up for the bus journey. It's impossible for the bus to stop en route for Freddie if he needs to, and it's the only way we have of keeping him dry until he arrives at school. Toileting Freddie takes about fifteen minutes. Then it's back downstairs where the other has hopefully finished feeding Henry. Sometimes, despite the overall we put on him, Henry is completely covered in milk and cereal and a complete change of uniform is needed. The boys have about eight full uniforms each to cater for the constant changes they require. Finally we get their coats on and the bus comes.

As soon as the boys are gone I change Henry's sheets, which will inevitably be wet or sicked on. He just sicks up the odd mouthful, but that's enough. It's rare that I don't have to change his bedding in the morning. When I get to Freddie's room my heart beats faster. I never know what I'll find. All I do know is that there will be at least an hour's work dealing with whatever is involved. He might have decided to empty the contents of every drawer and shelf on to the floor or peel off the wallpaper or, worse still, remove the plaster down to the brickwork which he so magnificently did on one recent occasion. The plaster repair cost £100 as he'd fully removed over a square metre, and all with a plastic Early Learning tool kit! Or he might – and this was the one I dreaded most – have done a poo and spread it everywhere.

By nine o'clock I feel fairly tired. No time for that – need to clean the house. We're on five floors and lugging the hoover up and down stairs doesn't fill me with joy. But it has to be done as we have Michael's business guests for dinner. Next, it takes forty minutes to an hour on average to do the laundry – the boys seem to pee and dribble an awful lot. Then it's another hour to prepare food that they 'will' in Henry's case, and 'can' in Freddie's, eat. I find it hard never being able to give them the odd fish finger or burger, as I often run out of imaginative culinary delights that will tempt them to eat. Michael used to quietly resent the fact that when it came to our supper he'd just get scrambled eggs on toast. He doesn't resent it any more.

By now my morning is rapidly disappearing. Just time for a caffeine boost and then it's upstairs to do the accounts for the Henry Spink Foundation and to answer all the messages, letters and emails to the Foundation from parents. I can empathise with all the callers. We have one thing in common, and that's exhaustion!

I grab a quick sandwich, gulp it down and head for the supermarket. I don't feel like preparing a dinner party and I can't think what to cook that won't involve me hopping up and down every ten minutes with a cooking timer or, most importantly, piles of washing up. The guests are due at eight. Hopefully they'll be a bit late, which will give me time to get the boys into bed – not that Freddie will stay – and get the house back into some semblance of order.

I rush back from the supermarket and hurriedly prepare most of the meal. Once the boys are home I'm on full-time duty and nothing else can be done while they're awake.

Feeding, bathing and toileting the boys takes two to three hours every evening, if we're lucky. Henry usually sits for at least forty minutes on the loo and someone needs to sit with him at all times because he can unexpectedly fit. He likes to be entertained, so we read to him.

By 7.30 we've got the boys into bed and Sharon goes home. I rush downstairs, praying Freddie will stay in his room during my preparation time and watch a video. I just don't need him emptying out all the drawers in my bedroom at this point, and I don't have time to watch him. I throw on a suit and Michael arrives home just before our guests. It's Friday night and I'm praying the guests won't stay too late.

Amazingly, Freddie only comes downstairs three times and is fairly easily persuaded back to bed. The guests finally leave at 12.30, which I suppose is not too bad. If I'm lucky we'll have cleared up and be in bed by 1 a.m. Whenever we have guests I know the kids will wake through the night. Perhaps I just notice it more. I remember on one occasion after a late night, and then having to get up for Freddie, who was choking, at about 3 a.m., I blacked out. I think I heard my head hit the ground before passing out. Michael thought it was Freddie pulling books off the shelf as he hadn't heard me get up. I don't know how long I lay there.

The boys are up at 6 a.m. Saturday morning. The same arduous day begins all over again, but this time there's no carer and no school, it's just Michael and me, facing the prospect of round-the-clock care for the next forty-eight hours.

We decided to approach Wandsworth directly, and they assessed us and decided we needed ten hours' help a week. Five hours for each boy – one carer in the morning and one in the evening five days a week. This was based on the assumption that I was always to be the other carer, which gave me no break at all. Inadequate as this was, it was better than nothing and we asked to go ahead. Wandsworth costed the ten hours at £70 and then means-tested us to decide what our contribution should be. The figure they came up with was £80. Since this was calculated as a percentage of Michael's salary, we were in the ludicrous position of being asked to pay more than the cost of the service we were already getting. It was better value for us to continue paying for Sharon ourselves, and Wandsworth tried to close the file on us for a third time.

The reality of what we needed was in any case far more

than ten hours' help a week. We also needed help at weekends and some respite care. By Sunday evenings we both felt at breaking point – we were becoming totally worn out by the harsh regime. We knew other families who were getting the right level of support, but, try as we might, we could not get it for ourselves. We felt as though we were banging our heads against a brick wall.

I was beginning to feel at an all-time low about the way we were being treated. I had read of the fantastic services offered in Scandinavia for the disabled, and felt extremely envious of people living in countries where civil and human rights were respected and upheld. I'd read the Carers' Act and the Children's Act and was appalled at how they could be flouted – they were as useless as the Code of Practice for Special Education which we'd already discovered to be a joke. We could access none of the help we needed and had finally managed to discover that we were entitled to.

It seemed like a bizarre irony to us that if at any stage we decided to put our boys into care it would cost the government £250,000 a year to look after them. We could choose to wash our hands of all responsibility and the state would be forced to take over. Yet because we chose to keep our children and care for them ourselves we were denied the help we needed. Sometimes it felt as though we were being punished for the choice we had made. Couldn't someone out there see that, by giving us the relatively inexpensive help we needed, the government would save money and we would all benefit?

For years I had been fighting tooth and nail with social services to get a ramp put outside our house. When the boys arrived home from school every day I had to pull Freddie up the three stairs to the front door and then carry him down the five stairs at the back of the hall to the kitchen. I would then go back, take Henry out of his wheelchair and repeat this process. Then I had to go back and carry the wheelchair into the house.

Finally, ten years after we had first applied for one, the council gave us a ramp. It cost them £2,000 and we couldn't get it to fit. Perhaps it was just as well, as the two halves of the ramp weighed more than the boys did. How could they expect me to fold up and carry two 15-foot metal ramps in and out of the house twice a day? If we left them outside they'd be stolen in five minutes.

I spent the next six months threatening Wandsworth that I'd sell the ramp if someone didn't come and replace it with something that worked. Finally the company that made the ramp came back to have a look. We carried the two halves out and they magically assembled them into one functioning ramp – a feat we had not been able to manage despite many attempts.

It was decided that, as the two halves of the ramp were far too heavy for me to cart in and out of the house four times a day, they should be permanently screwed together and chained to the wall. Fair enough. But there was, of course, a hitch. The ramp had a gradient of one-in-six when it should have been one-in-twelve. If the postman slipped on it he or she could sue; therefore we could not leave it outside.

Wandsworth's conclusion? I should continue to carry Henry, Freddie and the wheelchair up and down the stairs while the ramp lay useless in the cellar.

By now it was almost time for the summer holidays and I was feeling battle-weary. Being so incredibly tired all the time made me ratty, and the constant pointless battling for any small thing which might make our lives easier was exhausting and demoralising. I was afraid that I was no longer capable of being a good mother. I wondered how I'd manage to cope with the long summer break without a single day off. I felt I was quite likely to die of a heart attack or have a nervous breakdown before we got to September.

Henry had fallen on his teeth so often that one front tooth was broken and the other shunted out of place. After a three-month wait his appointment came up towards the end of the summer term and I took him to the hospital's orthodontic section. When we got there I was directed down a flight of stairs to the waiting room. I asked if there was a lift and the receptionist, who barely looked up from her computer screen, said, 'No.' So I jogged Henry's wheelchair down the stairs, praying it wouldn't slip, only to be informed that he needed an X-ray and that the X-ray department was back upstairs. I dragged the wheelchair back up, panting with the exertion, found the X-ray department and was sent to the waiting area.

It was very noisy and my heart sank. Henry, being extremely noise-sensitive, began to howl and everyone spent the next hour staring at us. Despite the fact that this happened all the time, I still hated it.

Eventually it was our turn. We went into a small X-ray room where a technician asked Henry to stand up, put his head in a machine and hold it perfectly still for two minutes while the machine circled his head. I explained that Henry, as he could plainly see, was in a wheelchair and therefore couldn't stand independently, let alone stay still. To which he replied, 'We only do normal people.' Why couldn't they have told me that an hour and a half ago? I returned to the orthodontist, heaving Henry down the stairs again, to be told that disabled kids couldn't have braces. At that point I gave up, dragged Henry up the stairs again and took him back to school for the afternoon.

It wasn't often that I allowed myself the luxury of tears, but that night I wept. Surrounded by dirty dishes, dirty clothes and heaps of paperwork waiting to be sorted, I sat in the kitchen, a cup of tea growing cold on the table in front of me, and bawled my eyes out. The sheer bloody unfairness of life felt overwhelming. I felt furious with everyone; the uncaring orthodontist, the people who stared at us in the waiting room, the awful au pairs, the people who parked in our disabled bay, everyone who worked for the council, and anyone else I could think of who didn't care or wouldn't help.

Why me? What had I done to deserve this? What kind of a karmic botch-up must I have made of another life to have landed this little lot? It was hard to believe in any kind of God who would let this happen. I loved my boys fiercely and passionately, but there were moments when I hated the fact that they weren't like other children and grieved for the dreams I'd had to let go of along the way.

That night I felt close to despair. Every step of the way, for the past fourteen years, had been a struggle. At that moment I wanted to throw in the towel, put my hands up and say, 'OK, I've had it. Enough.' I wanted to, but I couldn't, and deep down I knew I never would. Even in those tortured, painful moments of grief and overwhelmingness, a small voice somewhere inside me would say, 'Come on! Wipe your nose and get back on your feet. You're not giving up.'

The next morning I received a call, out of the blue, from Professor Ramachandran. Did he never forewarn anyone of his visits? He was in London for one day and he wanted to meet Henry. I suggested we meet at Michael's gallery. Michael had now set up on his own, selling antique and reproduction Eastern art. I felt sick all morning. What if he took one look at Henry and said, 'You must be kidding – I can't help someone that disabled.' How would I cope with rejection?

It was a boiling hot day and Michael's gallery felt like a furnace – or perhaps that was just me. My heart was racing. When he arrived, Professor Ramachandran, Michael and I sat down and talked for about two and a half hours. He didn't take his eyes off Henry once. I couldn't tell what he was thinking, and I'm grateful for that. He said he had some ideas and wanted to organise new MRI scans. More waiting. I'd heard it all before. But perhaps this time something would happen.

I survived the summer, but only just. Perhaps I was getting older or perhaps the cumulative effect of the constant lifting, sleepless nights and scarcity of breaks to recharge my batteries was taking its toll, but it was our hardest summer so far. Sharon was still with us, but one part-time helper wasn't enough and Michael was forced to take the whole summer off work to help care for the boys. This meant he was once again struggling against huge odds to keep his business going and make us enough money to live on. The knife-edge we balanced on seemed ever more perilous.

Once we were back in London and the boys were back at school I set about trying to raise some funds for the Foundation. I asked Alan Titchmarsh if he'd do a fund-raising evening for us. He happily agreed to do 'An Evening with . . .' at which he would tell funny personal anecdotes. The tickets were titled 'Champagne Reception and Entertainment, Tales from a Garden, with Alan Titchmarsh MBE'. The event was to be held on 6 December and I had to sell three hundred tickets in two months. It would take place during our poster campaign: a hundred were to be displayed across London in November, December and January.

The Foundation staff had worked tirelessly to set up a helpline and we were preparing to be inundated with calls. We were already receiving dozens of emails and calls every week from parents searching for help and advice. How many more would a giant poster campaign bring? I must admit to having been rather nervous – it was one hell of a responsibility.

The whole process of getting the poster campaign organised had been an awesome task. Three hundred students had entered the competition to design our poster. Their reward would be seeing their poster displayed across London – no mean achievement for a budding designer. I was one of a team of seven professionals judging the posters, which initially presented in miniature form and displayed in a large hall in London. I arrived early and started to wander round, deeply grateful that I was on my own. Completely bowled over with waves of unexpected emotion, I instantly felt like weeping. Three hundred students had thought up incredibly creative and unique images, all honouring the Henry Spink Foundation and ultimately my boys. It felt like the culmination and, at last, recognition of all my hard work – I was overwhelmed and very humbled.

The moment I walked through the door I had spotted the winner. It was in fact a series of four posters. The first was a very lush and vivid jungle scene. Handwritten in white pen across the top, with a large arrow pointing somewhere into the jungle, were the words: 'Your child's treatment was discovered here.' In the bottom corner, similarly, was: 'You'll discover it here', with a large arrow pointing to our contact details. The other three in the series ran along the same lines. They were simple, visually appealing and effective. After four hours' deliberation three finalists were chosen, with this series of four in first place. Everyone agreed it was the winner.

Next, Maiden Outdoor, who had donated the sites for the campaign, had to get me a single poster developed in time to organise a photo shoot with, we hoped, all our Patrons standing in front of it. It had to be done fast, because the actual launch was only a few days away. Alan Titchmarsh, Alastair Stewart and Felicity Kendal could make it for the press day; Darcey Bussell was away. I felt lucky to get three of them to agree. Maiden had picked a good site in Kennington, south London, for the shoot. It was an extremely proud moment for me when my Patrons stood in front of the poster and the press snapped away. I found it even more incredible when a week later, driving round London, I started spotting our posters – it sent shivers down my spine every time I saw one.

As soon as the posters went up we were, as anticipated, inundated with requests for information. A clear pattern was rapidly emerging. We were besieged by parents wanting information in four categories: autism, developmental delay, ADHD (hyperactivity) and behavioural problems. These four far outweighed any other enquiry.

The cost of paying the additional staff we needed to handle the incoming calls, plus the extra printing costs and postage, added up to far more than we had left in the kitty. Alan's evening was fundamental to our survival, so I was delighted when I sold the last of the tickets. Christie's had sponsored the champagne and Kyle, a good friend of mine, had cajoled a bunch of generous art dealers into sponsoring the other costs. This meant that the ticket sales would be all profit for the Foundation.

Caroline Mitchell, Alan's PA, contacted us to say that he was nervous about what he should wear. I couldn't stop laughing – I wondered how on earth someone so famous could worry about what they should wear. It just showed how very down to earth and unspoilt he was. I'm not sure whether it was because he was performing to a posh audience at Christie's or because the Duchess of Gloucester was supporting the evening and would be sitting in the front row. Either way I said he should relax and wear jeans if he wanted – no one would judge him!

Darcey Bussell and Felicity Kendal both came to

support the evening. With three major celebrities and a royal I knew I'd have no problems in getting the press there. I remember standing at the top of the grand stairs with Darcey and Felicity on either side and the paparazzi snapping away. Tomorrow, I thought, I shall be doing six loads of laundry and heaving my children up and down the front steps once again. No danger of my feet leaving the ground!

The evening was a great success. Our producer and photographer friend Tina Stallard had produced a wonderful series of pictures of four disabled children, including Henry and Freddie. She had won a very prestigious award with them and had asked me if she could exhibit them at Christie's on the evening. They were stunningly good shots with simple, heart-rending captions underneath that said it all. There was not a dry eye in the house. The photographs were hanging just outside the main room where Alan – who settled for a suit and tie in the end – would be giving his talk. All three hundred guests had already been ushered into the main room and asked to take their seats before the Duchess arrived. As I showed her the photographs she became so engrossed in them that our poor guests were left waiting in silent anticipation for quite some time!

When the evening finally began, Alan's stories were hilarious and everyone roared with laughter. I was delighted to see so many happy faces. Afterwards we had a sumptuous dinner at a lovely restaurant in St James's. We were a merry little party of six: Alan and his wife Alison, Caroline, Alan's PA, and her husband Neil, plus Michael and myself. We relaxed and laughed throughout dinner – relief all round that the event had gone so well.

Back home, I had still had no word from Ramachandran, so I tried emailing him to see if he'd got anywhere with organising the scans. He replied that he hadn't got anywhere with organising them in America. I emailed him back reminding him that he'd said London, not the USA. He apologised and said he'd try to organise the scans after Christmas. I could have screamed.

Christmas came and went and I tried in vain to contact Ramachandran. After a time I gave up and asked Michael if he could call his good friend Bill in California to see whether he could reach him more easily. Unfortunately Bill didn't have any luck either, but he did have a friend called Wally who had a friend called Jim, a neuro-anatomist at the University of California at Irvine. Jim had agreed to look at Henry's notes.

Jim immediately responded to my emails and asked me to send over current MRI scans. I sighed and explained I didn't have any, nor a paediatrician to set them up. All I had were scans taken when Henry was three years old – somewhat out of date. He said OK, send the old ones. I packaged them up and sent them off.

A week later I received an email from Jim. He'd looked at the scans. 'There is one slight "interesting" feature that appears to me to be a bit different,' he said.

Chapter 17

Jim discussed Henry's scans with a raft of different experts in California. The conclusion was that they needed a more up-to-date MRI scan. My heart sank. I would need to find a friendly paediatrician to refer Henry. The last one I had gone to had said, 'Don't you think it's time you let go, dear?' How easy would it be for me to get a referral when I was up against this sort of attitude?

I wished I could go back to David Hall, the kind and caring paediatrician who had visited us when Henry was small and afterwards carried Henry's notes around with him. Sadly, he had retired, and no one had taken any real interest in Henry's condition since. I was determined, though. If Jim had seen something in Henry's scan which warranted further investigation then I was going to get him the scan – however many doors I had to bang on.

I did find another paediatrician, but it took many months plus various emails from Jim to the person concerned to get our scan. The paediatrician thought Americans 'do tests willy-nilly and don't know what to do with the results anyway'. I never mentioned my vision for Henry, as I knew this would label me a complete nutter. I just kept on and on asking for the scan until he finally agreed, probably out of desperation to be rid of me!

While I was trying to get Henry's scan sorted we approached the Disability Law Service, a charity that helped families in our position with free legal advice and representation. We asked if they could advise us on how to get more help from social services, as so far our every attempt to get help had resulted in a brush-off. Charlotte, the DLS's charming solicitor, explained that we would have to go through a formal complaints procedure before we could go to court to try to obtain an appropriate help package. We agreed to go ahead with the complaints procedure, which was to drag out for months.

I asked Charlotte if they had an education specialist. She referred me to another solicitor, Jo, and I asked her whether a group action by a number of families against Wandsworth's Special Educational Needs department would be possible. Jo thought it was feasible, but it had never been done before and she wanted to seek a barrister's advice. I rang Gavin Millar to ask if he'd meet us, and he generously agreed. Gavin thought that the clearest route was to go for a formal complaint to the Secretary of State for Education. He suggested we find twenty-five families – a number that couldn't be ignored – and get as much publicity as we could. This might eventually shift ministers into addressing the flaws in the system. Unfortunately the Disability Law Service said they were too small to be able to take it on and gracefully backed out. This left me without a solicitor.

Our good friend Tina Stallard had repeated our story to a member of the BBC's *Panorama* team. I was excited: this was exactly the kind of coverage we needed to make a real impact. Disappointingly, they decided we weren't right because too many of us had middle-class accents. The irony was that most people with the 'right' accents were on benefits and were therefore automatically entitled to legal aid. As home owners, we were entitled to nothing. But wasn't suffering the same for everyone, no matter what their accent? Surely disability has no class – it affects all of us equally.

The *Panorama* reporter wasn't to be moved – we should have, at the very least, an ethnic minority group, preferably unable to speak English. We just weren't politically correct enough. So that was that. But before bowing out the reporter gave me an introduction to a well-known solicitor. I was grateful, and this solicitor agreed to take the case on. We were in business again.

Next we had to sort out which families would take part in the action. Some of those we were in touch with were too terrified or too traumatised and exhausted to get involved with any form of group action. They were afraid of being punished or singled out by Wandsworth. I hired our ex-nanny Angela, now a paralegal, to start gathering the names of families with a legitimate case who would commit to the group complaint.

Cassandra Jardine from the *Telegraph* had approached me about doing another article: she wanted to come back and find out what had happened. In her update she mentioned that since Freddie's birth I had recorded all my thoughts on tape as an audio diary. Her editor came back and said could I write up my tape diaries as a five-thousand-word magazine feature? I agreed, and began the task of listening to the sixty or so tapes I had made over the years. It was painful and not

at all cathartic. So much of what I had said was an-
guished, bewildered, angry and full of suffering. It was
peculiar listening to it all, knowing as I now did the way
events had unravelled. It all seemed so cruel and sad. I
was also shocked at how my memory of events had
edited the past. Without the tapes to remind me of what I
had really felt I would have painted a very different
picture, cutting out a lot of the rawest and most painful
parts.

The feature was eventually published, illustrated with
several nice photographs of Michael and me with the
boys. As soon as it came out we were once again
inundated with letters offering to do our laundry, fix
our kids' teeth, baby-sit and go shopping for us. The
outpouring of generosity we received was quite overwhelming, and a wonderful reminder of how much
goodness there is in the world.

I'd written about the difficulties of going on holiday
and the terrible extra expenses that were involved with
two disabled children. It automatically meant two
extra full adult fares for the carers we would need
to take with us, salaries at £10 per hour (double at
night) and extra rooms. A woman contacted us anon-
ymously, giving us only her first name and asking us
not to pass it on, and said she'd like to give us £10,000
to pay for a holiday. Touched as we were by her offer,
we felt daunted by the prospect of spending such a vast
amount of money on a single holiday – it seemed far
too extravagant. Besides which, we didn't have any
carers to come with us at the time and couldn't face
taking two total strangers. We asked if we could take

her offer up later, when we had appropriate help in place, and she agreed.

I had also written about pieces of equipment we needed but could not get through social services. I had written in one diary entry:

Henry is now nearly too heavy to lift; it can only be a matter of time before one or both of us puts our back out, and what happens then? Freddie is even heavier. We desperately need a bath hoist or a bath with an integrated seat, and a ceiling hoist to get Henry in and out of bed. The occupational therapist has been round and agrees; an independent assessor is amazed that we have managed this long without this gear. But, according to Wandsworth council, anything fixed in place, which covers all the above equipment, is counted as a home improvement (what a joke) and so is subject to the same means-test used if you are adding thousands to the value of your house. The equipment is only for the benefit of the boys, yet it is the parents not the children who are assessed. We simply do not have the money; our fight over the boys' education has seen to that. After paying for the carers and the mortgage and all the other vast expenses that go with disabled children we don't have heaps over, so I doubt that we will be able to pay the percentage – up to 8 per cent of our income – the government wants. The result: we will not have any equipment. What happens when we injure ourselves, do the boys go into care? Does the council provide someone to lift them?

A kindly soul who read this entry offered us the use of his deceased wife's hoist to get Henry into bed. He even covered the cost of the installation.

The solicitor who had been recommended by the

Panorama researcher was not responding to my calls and I was getting worried. But by another wonderful coincidence a friend of Michael's, Vanessa Salmon, happened to be great mates with a senior partner in a major negligence law firm, Irwin Mitchell. She was happy to introduce me to her and she passed us on to another senior partner, Andrew Lockley, who specialised in education. Andrew listened to the saga and immediately suggested we meet. He rapidly proved to be a canny and effective lawyer.

When he came round to see us he looked at all the scribblings Angela and I had done on each of the families and immediately told us to dump the idea of a formal complaint, as it would sit in a minister's bottom drawer for ever. Instead, we should take the council to court for 'failure of provision'. At the tribunal Henry had been given a statement clearly allocating him occupational therapy, speech therapy and SENMAC, a form of communication and swimming. But even though they had been awarded, Wandsworth had failed to provide any of them: Freddie too had not been provided with the paltry fifteen minutes of speech therapy he had been awarded by his tribunal panel.

Most parents can't bear to have to return to court after battling through a tribunal. They settle for whatever part of the provision they actually get. We were the same: we had felt too shattered to try any longer and had decided that having got Henry's school place we would let the therapies go. Now Andrew was saying that going to the High Court on failure of provision was the only route, not only to get our therapies but to pursue my aim of getting the law changed. We'd have to gather our twenty-five families and then get their schools to put in writing that the provisions required in the statements were not being met. If we could show systematic failure to provide what had been specified, Wandsworth would be investigated and made to behave properly. It was a hell of a task, but I felt it must be done. We knew so many children who were missing out on vital therapies and treatments – perhaps if a large enough group stepped forward we'd be able to change things for everyone. That was what I wanted.

I set up a meeting for parents at Battersea town hall in south London. About thirty-five couples attended. The atmosphere was electric. One particularly vociferous parent sat in the corner heckling whenever he could get a word in. 'When are we —ing going to sue them?' he rasped. Backed by Andrew and three other lawyers, Michael explained what was going to be involved in order to do just that. At the end of the meeting eighteen sets of parents willing to take part signed forms applying for legal aid on behalf of their children. None of the families would be able to proceed without legal aid, and as the children were named in the case they were the ones who must have the aid. This presented problems – obtaining legal aid for children is extremely difficult, as parents are usually held liable for their costs. But Andrew thought he could find a way round the law.

Some of the families were still reluctant to take part. Over the next few weeks Angela and I spent hours on the phone cajoling parents and explaining that if they participated we might be able to change things for everyone.

We also had to check out the facts for each family very carefully, to be certain they were accurate and fitted with our case. Eventually we found another seven families who fitted the bill and were willing to take part. We had our twenty-five.

Soon after my diary extracts came out in the *Telegraph* we were contacted by an independent TV production company. One of the producers I met told me that her husband was a negligence lawyer and suggested that we had a case for negligence because of the circumstances of Freddie's birth. Tina Stallard, our producer friend, had once asked me whether I thought Freddie had brain damage because he had been deprived of oxygen for the first twenty minutes after his birth. At that time we weren't ready to accept that he might be brain-damaged, but since then we had gradually come to terms with it. Now it was being suggested that the hospital, by not spotting his condition on the scans and having oxygen and life-support equipment ready at his birth, was at fault.

I talked to the lawyer, who asked a lot of questions and then said he thought we had a strong negligence case. Andrew Lockley agreed to take it on alongside our other cases, but warned that this kind of action usually took several years. At this stage we were already so immersed in legal wrangles that taking on another didn't feel very dramatic. We thought we might as well go ahead and see what happened – we hadn't much to lose. We knew it would be a long-term affair and that for now our energies would be expended on the more immediate cases – the group action and our fight to get social services to help us. But we felt that it was important to battle on to put right all the wrongs we could, to stand up not only for ourselves but for all the families who had suffered in similar ways. If the doctors had been negligent, surely this too should be exposed.

By now, after all the press coverage, families from all over England had contacted us. I remember one distraught mother who could hardly speak for sobbing. Her twelve-year-old son was autistic and had never been to school. Her borough didn't have an appropriate school, so she wanted to send him to one that was out of borough. But her local education authority insisted she'd have to go to tribunal. As a single mother she simply couldn't afford to face a battle like that. Neither could she bear to send her son to a totally inappropriate school. So she had kept him at home for five years.

Another family whose two children were dying contacted me to say they'd been forced to go to tribunal over their education, while the children quietly deteriorated during the long wait. The LEA withdrew their case the day before the tribunal was due, allowing them to go to the school of their choice but too late to save the thousands of pounds the family had spent on lawyers and reports. Another mum who got in touch had two disabled boys and a younger son dying of leukaemia. She and her husband had also been forced to go to tribunal over their two older boys' education. They had won, but only after going through hell.

These were just three of the many families who got in touch with us, and hearing their stories made us feel that we must keep fighting no matter what. Every battle won would be for all of us, for all the parents and children who had suffered from the callousness and indifference of education authorities and social services all over the country. We felt that someone had to stand up and say, 'Enough.'

A journalist called Caroline Scott phoned to ask if she could write about me, the boys and the Henry Spink Foundation for a women's magazine. Caroline told me that she also wrote for the *Sunday Times*. 'I'll do the feature if you write one on my education campaign for the *Sunday Times* magazine,' I told her. She agreed to ask the editor of the magazine, and by a remarkable coincidence it turned out that she had a special needs son in Wandsworth and was having a tough time getting appropriate provision for him. She readily agreed to the feature and allocated several pages of the magazine to it.

Soon after this we were approached by an independent radio production company. Laura, the producer, asked if they could do a feature on us for the BBC's Radio 4. It was to be called *Life with Henry and Freddie*. She wanted to base it on my audio diaries and to include interviews with people who knew me. I suggested she interview Tina Stallard and Michael's youngest brother, Sandy. Tina had followed our every move and filmed or photographed us over many years, and Sandy had always been very sympathetic.

The programme received much praise and was 'choice of the week' in virtually all the papers. Several friends rang us afterwards to say they'd had to stop their cars on the motorway to listen to it. Few were left with a dry eye. Soon afterwards Laura rang me with great excitement to say it was being nominated for a Sony Award – the radio world's equivalent of the Oscars.

However, alongside the highs of the radio programme's success, the generous response to my diary feature and the news that we could go ahead with our group action against Wandsworth, there was one real low. Our complaints procedure against Wandsworth's social services department was still going ahead and it was really getting us down. We felt it was right to fight to change the law concerning disabled children's educational rights, having been through the battles we'd had over the boys' education. We believed deeply in our cause and we hoped a successful outcome would change things for many families, not just the twenty-five taking part with us in the action. But the case against social services simply wore us out. It seemed exhausting, needless and unfair. Why couldn't we get the basic provision we were entitled to without such a long, painful battle?

Over the next few months, as we ground our way through the complaints procedure against social services, there were some slow but steady improvements in the care package we received from social services. In several stages, Wandsworth increased the boys' care hours from the original ten a week to two each morning and three each evening for each boy. They also gave us an additional two hours twice a week, so that we could take the boys on outings after school.

This meant that Sharon's hours would be increased and we would be given another carer. She came via the Special People agency which I had found and which Wandsworth agreed to use. Her name was Eva and she was sweet, generous, calm and very reliable. Soon afterwards Sharon left and Janet, our old nanny, came back into our lives. She arrived out of the blue and we were thrilled to see her. The bond between Janet and Freddie was still just as strong. She had split up with her boyfriend and wanted to work for us again, so I suggested she join Special People and work for us alongside Eva, which she did. For the next few months this arrangement worked incredibly well.

Not long before Henry reached his fifteenth birthday we were finally given our first respite weekend. We were told that we would be allowed eight respite weekends a year. This, of course, was wonderful compared to no weekends at all. But the sixteen nights' respite these weekends would give us still fell far short of Wandsworth's own guidelines, which stated that parents should have a minimum of fifty-six days' and nights' respite per year. And we were still not allowed any weekend or holiday care. Why were we, who had two disabled children and so needed help even more, refused it?

We felt we must go ahead with the legal action. The improved package was certainly a help, but it just didn't go far enough. We hoped that if we kept going with the action we would be given our full entitlement to help without having to go as far as a court case.

Having already been through many intrusive and unpleasant assessments, we were told that we now had to go through one more. Having our home and space invaded once again was not easy and we felt the assessor was far from sympathetic. One classic statement she made in her assessment was that Mr and Mrs Spink often looked incredibly exhausted. But instead of recommending that we receive adequate care for the boys she suggested that our exhaustion would be reduced if we had a little counselling! We were referred to the children's psychiatric department at St George's Hospital and were obliged to take the appointment. If we didn't, they could say we weren't being willing participants.

We met a lovely psychiatrist who chatted to us for a couple of hours. By the end of the appointment he said he had learned a huge amount from us. He felt he couldn't really help us as our marriage was strong and we plainly communicated extremely well. This was true – we always discussed every aspect of our lives together. He agreed our need was for hours of care, not counselling, but said that we were welcome to visit him at any time. We wondered whether he would put all this in writing to Wandsworth.

When he received a copy of this latest assessment our solicitor suggested our only hope of getting an appropriate care package was to go ahead with court action. Wandsworth were plainly not going to meet our needs without a major fight.

By now life seemed to be one long round of legal battles, and the thought of court action was exhausting and dispiriting. I longed for it all to be over, for life to be peaceful and settled. I felt increasingly low, and finding the energy to care for the boys and look after the Foundation against this background was sometimes almost more than I could manage.

Even with the help we had, just taking the boys out anywhere was a major logistical nightmare. I remember a friend asking us to tea. I was delighted – it would be a rare treat. I told her I'd be bringing two carers, to which she responded, 'Oh, do you have to? It'll be much more fun if it's just us.' I sighed and explained that I couldn't even get out of the house with the boys without the help of two other people. Which meant, of course, that we could only go out when the helpers were there. At weekends we were trapped at home.

Michael and I both felt very down. We just couldn't understand why we must go to court to get the basic provision we were supposedly entitled to. We felt afraid that one or both of us would collapse with the stress and exhaustion of the battles we had to fight and caring for the boys. For a while our relationship plodded along in a vacuum of despair. It seemed that the authorities held all the cards, and we felt crushed by the reality of the boys' massive problems and what we were up against to help us to survive.

We cared for the boys on auto-pilot and I'm sure they knew it. Much as we loved them, we were unable to give them the energy or attention they needed and this only added to our worry. Was all this battling going to do the boys more harm than good in the end?

We questioned whether we should have just put Henry into Paddock and not cared that it was the wrong school. We wondered whether we should have put our kids into care. We wondered what we could have done differently that would have avoided our current situation. Every which way we turned we seemed to hit a blank wall. There was no right answer. We felt we were being destroyed by a system supposedly there to help us. It almost seemed funny.

For a while I hit a real period of depression, so bad that there were days when I wished the boys and I were dead. Perhaps then, I felt, Michael could have a chance of a decent life. Somehow, deep down, I had believed that social services would help us without a court fight. Now I knew they wouldn't, and it hit me hard. I had always believed in miracles, and in a path of justice. We both had. I felt that one day someone would stand up and put right all that was so wrong, for us and for other families, in the treatment of our children. For a while this belief, which had kept me going through so much, seemed to sink without trace. But thankfully it was still there, lurking deep down, and eventually it resurfaced and with it my fighting spirit. I knew that I would not – must not – let the system beat me.

I dreamed that one day we'd get help with the boys at weekends so that we wouldn't feel dead by Sunday evenings. I dreamed that Michael would have the right to work. I wanted to see him fulfil his potential and use to the full the incredible expertise he had acquired after all those years in the art world. I dreamed we could earn a salary that would support us and pay the mortgage without endless hours of worry. I dreamed that I could have some freedom one day to pursue my own path – I had ambitions too. I dreamed my children would be happy. It was these dreams that kept me going.

In December 2002 Henry was booked into the Atkinson Morley's Hospital to have his MRI scans. I could hardly believe that after nine months of effort we'd finally got our referral. All went incredibly smoothly and we were out of hospital in a matter of hours. The

scans were sent to Jim at UCI in California. As I packaged those hard fought for scans I packed up fifteen years
of hopes and dreams. There are no words to describe
how I felt – I knew that if there was to be a miracle, the
key to it was in this small parcel. It represented a small
but clear light at the end of a very long, dark tunnel, and
all I could do was to pray.

As soon as he received the scans Jim emailed me to say
that these were much clearer images and he thought
Henry might be treatable with drugs. I didn't understand
much of his email – his analysis of Henry's brain anat-
omy was way beyond my comprehension. But I understood one thing very clearly: he was saying there was
hope for Henry.

My head spun. I read and reread the email, then
phoned Michael and read it to him. At that moment
everything else – the legal battles, the exhaustion, the
misery and the endless days and nights of caring for the
boys – faded. This was it. This man, this kind, caring man
we had never even met, was telling us, quite clearly, that
he believed Henry's condition was treatable with drugs.
One word, 'treatable', held the promise of all that I had
dreamed of for so long. I said a silent prayer of thanks for
everyone and everything that had led me to this point.

Jim now wanted a PET scan. An MRI scan was like an
X-ray and a PET scan was a functionality test – it showed
you how the brain was operating. I could see the logic in
getting this done, but I knew it would be another nightmare trying to organise it. I contacted my paediatrician,
who said he'd never referred anyone for one of these
scans before. I felt like weeping down the phone. Why

could no one find an ounce of compassion or forward thinking in this country? Was it always to be a battle? I persuaded Jim to email our paediatrician and explain exactly why he wanted this information. After all, this was coming from a top American neuroanatomist – surely it wouldn't be a problem?

Eventually, with much reluctance, we were given a referral to the Middlesex Hospital. After a few weeks my paediatrician rang to say the Middlesex had refused to do it and that he would refer us instead to St Thomas's. He suggested I ring them after a week or so. I did, and St Thomas's said I should ring back the next week to make the appointment. I could hardly believe it.

But when I rang St Thomas's the next week they said, 'Sorry, we can't do it.' Henry would need a general anaesthetic because he couldn't lie still. They only did general anaesthetics for scans one day a month, which meant they could scan only a handful of people a year. These scans were reserved for cancer patients. In their opinion Henry didn't merit a scan. I asked if we could go on a waiting list, but they said he would never be a priority. Internally I screamed with rage – what could I do? When I informed Jim he simply couldn't believe it. Scans like this are commonplace in America, where anyone can be referred for one very simply.

I was damned if I would give up. I typed 'PET scan UK' into the Internet. Up came the Cromwell Hospital. I emailed them – could Henry have a PET scan? He needed a general anaesthetic – would that be OK? And how much did it cost? Back came the answer. Yes, Henry could have the scan and it would cost approximately

£2,000. I gulped, but said OK. Michael telephoned our anonymous reader from the *Telegraph* and said we needed to pay for a scan for Henry instead of a holiday – would that be OK? She immediately told us to go ahead.

We then received an email from the doctor in charge at the Cromwell. A paediatric referral was adequate for the NHS but not for the private sector – we needed a neurologist's referral, which we didn't have. Professor Jim Fallon, although a leading neuroanatomist, wouldn't do either – it had to be a neurologist. I decided to contact Professor Ramachandran, who was a neurologist. He immediately sent a referral. The Cromwell now had a paediatrician's referral, a neuroanatomist's referral and a neurologist's referral, and we were ready to pay. I just needed confirmation of the date.

We received another email from a doctor at the Cromwell. He wouldn't do the scan on Henry, nor would he give a reason why he'd refused. I sat and wept. Our one chance of a breakthrough was being denied. The cruelty and unfairness of it all threatened to overwhelm me.

I emailed Jim and told him that we had been refused the PET scan by both the NHS and the private health sector. Two minutes later he emailed me back: 'Come over here.'

My heart raced. 'Why not?' I thought.

Chapter 18

Michael emailed our anonymous benefactor and explained what had happened. She said, 'Don't worry. I'll pay for the trip.' We planned to travel to California at the end of May, when the boys had their half-term. This was two months away and there was masses to organise.

Janet had left us. She had come to Cornwall with us over Christmas and again for the boys' spring half-term in February, when she had an asthma attack. After four days she seemed so ill that I decided to call an ambulance. She returned to Scotland to recuperate, and although we hoped she would come back to us she didn't.

Then Jane came on the scene as our second carer. She radiated warmth and was one of the sunniest, funniest people we'd met. She was training to be a speech therapist and holding down a pub job too, yet she often offered to step in and help us for free on top of the hours she was paid for. We now had Jane and Eva working as a team, and we felt blessed to have them. They adored the boys and the boys adored them in return. We hadn't had carers like this for years. I asked them if they would come with us to America and they both said yes. We couldn't believe our luck. Going with two such incredibly special people would make all the difference. With her typical generosity Jane didn't assume we'd pay her and asked how much the ticket would cost. She was thrilled to discover that the trip would be paid for and she would be paid a salary as well.

The hope of a breakthrough for Henry prompted me to contact my sister Cara. We hadn't spoken for almost five years, since my father's death, and I missed her. My father had abandoned us in childhood and I was damned if he'd succeed in parting us with his death. We'd been so close as children; I often felt we'd only survived because we had one another. I wanted Cara to be part of Henry's healing, and I knew she would love to see the miracle unfold. My children have taught me, above all else, that love is what counts. So I emailed her and said I'd love to see her again. Cara was thrilled, and so was I when I heard from her. The prospect of seeing each other again after such a stupid, needless and pride-fuelled separation was wonderful. We agreed to meet in Richmond Park. My spirits soared.

Caroline Scott had finished writing her article and a delightful photographer came to take photos for it. I suggested we go to Wandsworth council's dump and place Henry in his wheelchair in the middle of a skip. This was what I felt Britain thought my child was fit for – the rubbish tip. We pulled it off, slipping into the dump and, with much laughter, managing to get Henry and his wheelchair into the middle of a huge heap of rubbish. Henry clearly thought it was hilarious too, and we got through the whole thing without getting caught.

Caroline's feature appeared over six pages of the *Sunday Times* magazine. She had catalogued Wandsworth's abuse of three families, and her last paragraph read:

> Imagine now that your disabled child is growing up fast. You're worried about his future, how he will cope when you're not there. You may have already spent 10 or 15 years in the system, fighting every step of the way for what little provision you have gained. You are alone. You are invisible. You have no voice at all. You know you have been lied to, given misinformation, a second-rate service. And yet there will be no criminal complaints procedure, no redress. If you do get up the strength to shout, to complain about what is being done, who do you think is going to hear? And more importantly, who do you think cares?

Before the feature went to print Caroline had tried to have a meeting with Baroness Ashton of Upholland – the minister responsible for the education of children with special educational needs – to try to discuss the issues raised in her feature. After persistently trying, with no response, she began to log her attempts to contact Baroness Ashton and even tried to set up a meeting through a contact of ours, Liz Astor's husband Lord Astor of Hever.

When the feature appeared a copy was sent to Baroness Ashton, who claimed that she had never been contacted by Caroline. Her letter to the editor of the *Sunday Times Magazine* also showed she hadn't the faintest clue about the issues in the feature. She claimed that the article did 'a disservice to the work of special schools, LEAs and mainstream schools' and declared herself 'proud of the work that is underway to create a more inclusive system . . .' and 'committed to providing a high-quality, happy educational experience for every one of these young people'. Caroline sent me copies of Baroness Ashton's letter and the reply from the magazine's editor, Robin Morgan. I howled with laughter. Robin had written:

Dear Baroness Ashton

Thank you for your letter which raises several issues, not least (a) the suspicion that you did not read the article, (b) that you have been inaccurately informed, both of its content and the evidence it presented, (c) that someone is being deliberately untruthful, (d) that you have your head in the sand. To take your letter paragraph by paragraph:

1. You seem to be under the impression that the piece was about special schools. It was not. The investigation was about provision; particularly the gap that exists between what is spelled out as a legal entitlement in terms of provision for children with statements of special needs [or records of needs in Scotland] and what is often not provided for them by LEAs who must work within strict budgets. Without a doubt, the evidence is of families up and down the country being denied their legal right, stonewalled, ignored, manipulated, bullied and even lied to. That evidence is unequivocal – and your letter will outrage those families by seeking to brush aside their serious concerns.

I am surprised that you seem unaware that families who feel their children have been given inappropriate provision within mainstream or special schools, have to argue their case in a hostile system that drives them to the brink of emotional despair, ill health and financial ruin.

These are issues which these families could expect their elected representatives to take seriously. Instead they have to find a voice in the press. It will be of interest to them that their views and experience are so disregarded by you. It is not our article that does a disservice to special schools, LEAs or mainstream schools, it is the system you supervise.

2. By coincidence, we found it interesting that you rise in defence of special schools' fine work, quoting 'the crucial role they play' and your expectation of a report that will give them increasing 'support in the future'. Your statement flies in the face of facts; the borough we focussed on – Wandsworth – is in the process of closing some of its special schools. Wandsworth LEA is, of course, not alone in making these changes. It is interesting that you have asked for some research on special schools. We would like to see the report when it is ready.

3. You claim you 'would have been delighted to have been given the opportunity to make these points in person and to correct many of the factual inaccuracies in the article'. This doesn't wash. The facts are:

Caroline Scott tried many times to reach you over several weeks through the DfES. As her deadline approached and she still hadn't had a response from you, she began to keep a log. These records begin on the 27th January through to the 6th February and show a determined effort to reach you, the final log noting four calls in one day. She was assured that her messages had been delivered and there was no alternative route to take.

Of course, it is quite likely you were never told of our repeated requests. In which case one must question just how much crucial information is filtered before it reaches you, not just in terms of press interest but of the facts in Caroline Scott's article that you so readily dismiss. As for your attempt to negate the article, I note you have not backed up your claim of factual inaccuracies. We would like to offer you the opportunity of discussing these and the issues raised in our piece in an interview.

Yours sincerely
Robin Morgan
Editor, *Sunday Times Magazine*

This letter delighted all of us. Finally someone had openly stood up for us. 'Bravo!' was all I could say.

I had hoped that highlighting these cases in the press would somehow impress upon government ministers that there were serious flaws in the system. But there had been no official response to Caroline's feature and the answer to her question, 'Who do you think cares?' was patently clear. 'No one.'

I'd taken on this legal action because I truly believed it was the right thing to do. Naïvely, I thought that a High Court action would be the ultimate proof to the ministers that the system wasn't working. But the lack of response to the *Sunday Times* piece made me realise that there was nothing I could do to focus attention on the changes needed. Internally I wept with frustration. I wanted the injustices highlighted and rectified. I wanted a life free from legal wrangles. I felt I'd done my bit, and I wanted a politician to take the baton from me and get it sorted. I desperately wanted to move away from campaigning, back into my own orbit and helping my boys. But no one was willing to step in, and despite my weariness with the whole thing I vowed to continue. Whatever obstacles came my way I would face up to them. I would do whatever it took to change things.

Irwin Mitchell, our solicitors, told us that the first seven children in our group action had been granted legal aid. This was marvellous news, but we were told that it was now extremely likely that Wandsworth would settle the cases before they went to court. And indeed they did. This was so typical of their attitude: fight to the bitter end to avoid their duty, but when cornered provide what they should have provided in the first place. By settling before the High Court action Wandsworth had avoided any formal reprimand. Ironically, this annoyed the press far more than if they had gone to court. Several papers reported it, and *Private Eye* ran a piece called 'Educashun, Educashun, Educashun' which said it all. But still not a single politician stepped forward. Our action – and Wandsworth's response – had been the ultimate proof that the system was wholly corrupt. And no one gave a damn.

I knew I was not going to let it rest there. No doubt Wandsworth would also settle out of court with the other eighteen families, but I had come too far to give up. I felt a responsibility to the other families that Wandsworth had betrayed, and to my own children, to take this as far as I had to. I contacted Richard Howitt, our Euro MP, about the possibility of taking the matter to the European courts.

Simultaneously we were drawing to a close, or so we hoped, with social services' lack of provision for the boys. We had been granted legal aid, but the lawyer's reports were taking for ever to finalise and it became clear that they would not be ready to go to court before the end of term.

By now we were approaching crisis point financially. Because Michael and I had to be the full-time carers for every school holiday and half-term – thirteen weeks a year – Michael simply couldn't earn a proper living. His business was struggling and the point was fast approaching when we would no longer be able to pay our mortgage. If we didn't receive help to care for the boys over the coming summer holidays we would risk losing our house. We were sick with worry. I tried to have faith that all would be well, but in truth I felt afraid and abandoned.

The head of social services had been to see us. When we said we couldn't pay the mortgage if we didn't receive adequate care during the holidays he replied, 'We have no legal or moral duty to help keep you in work – when you are on benefits then we'll help.'

Michael thought it would be better to sell the house before we lost it and move to our cottage in Cornwall. I didn't want to. Cornwall was my place of escape, my retreat, the way I kept my sanity. It all felt horribly wrong, but our backs were against the wall. I couldn't believe we were being forced out of our home. We needed to be in London to earn a living. Michael's business was wholly dependent on being in London. All our clients came through London, and none would be prepared to travel three hundred miles west to see us. Michael knew this, but at this point he'd given up on being able to work and so it made no odds to him to move. He'd lost hope. I hadn't, but I couldn't see any other way out of the financial crisis we were in.

We visited the Cornish special needs schools and were amazed at how good they were. The staff smiled, the children were obviously very happy and the facilities were far better than anything we'd seen before. The boys were given places for September. We planned to put our London house on the market and move at the end of July, when the school term ended.

All I could do to stem the ever-growing fear within me was to concentrate on our forthcoming American trip. My vision for Henry was my only reality – something I had always had to hang on to. As had happened many times before, it kept me going when the waves seemed to be closing over my head. This vision – so strong, so clear, so consistent despite all the cynicism, doubts and put-downs I'd had over the years – was about to be tested. Would I be proved right?

The week before we were due to set off for the States the 'what if' syndrome hit me hard. For fifteen years I had been so certain that we would find a cure for Henry. What if I was wrong? What if they couldn't help him and I really was just an over-zealous, misguided mother? I heard the paediatrician's voice ringing in my ears once again: 'Don't you think it's time you let go, dear?' What if he and all the others who had questioned or discouraged my belief in my son's future were right? I had fought for so long to get to where I now was. Could I have been wrong?

By the time we were on the plane to Los Angeles I was calmer. What would be would be, and I would find a way to deal with it. After all, my instinct had got me this far and Jim Fallon wasn't inviting us over on a fool's errand – he knew this was a big deal for us.

Michael's father had prescribed Valium for Henry to take during the flight in case it all became too much. We'd gone on a flight to New York several years before and Henry, furious that he wasn't tucked up in bed, had hurled himself backwards and forwards for the entire trip. This had meant that several rows of seats had been slammed back and forth all night – we weren't too popular with the other passengers! And Freddie had suffered from a bout of gastro-enteritis. Definitely a flight to remember.

So the Valium was there just in case – but, thank goodness, Henry and Freddie behaved immaculately. Actually I felt sorely tempted to take it myself. Changing Henry in the loo was a highlight of this trip. I sat on the loo, Henry sat on my lap and Eva knelt on the floor changing him. A couple of air stewardesses hovered, asking if we needed any help. I really thought five in a British Airways loo would be taking the mile-high experience to new heights! Believe me, three was cosy enough. The BA crew were in fact amazing – every inch of the way we had been ushered past queues and they had announced our name over the tannoy so many times, offering help and assistance, that we felt like celebrities.

We had hired a seven-seater people-carrier for the other end. Getting six of us plus two wheelchairs, a beach buggy, several thousand nappies and six suitcases into it proved to be an extremely interesting exercise in ingenuity. We finally managed to get the doors shut and set off. Michael, who was driving, was the only person to have partial vision out of the car. In America most of the roads are on a grid formation which means driving in endless straight lines. Dull, but a blessing as Michael could hardly move his elbows to turn the wheel.

We had rented a bungalow for our stay. This was our first experience of living in one and, after a lifetime of carting the kids up and down several flights of stairs each day, it was sheer bliss. Even so, none of us could sleep, and by morning we had been awake for twenty-four hours. Despite this Jane and Eva were upbeat, energetic and enthusiastic. Not once did either complain – we couldn't believe our luck.

Jim had set up various medical appointments for our first day, starting at 8.30 a.m. and lasting all day. The hours passed in a blur – we saw many experts and nearly all donated their services for free. They were fascinated by Henry and couldn't understand why the British medical establishment had not been riveted too. They found it hard to believe that no doctor in Britain had shown the slightest bit of curiosity about why a child with a normal brain was not functioning at all. The Americans not only questioned this attitude but said it was downright negligent. We felt incredibly lucky and a little over-awed. The Americans' compassion and interest were something we had never experienced before.

Their facilities were also astounding. I couldn't believe how clean, orderly and attractive all the medical centres were. In my experience most British hospitals are pretty filthy. I've had to take the boys into disgusting toilets and sit with them in waiting rooms which look as though a herd of drunken soccer fans have waded through, smashing everything in sight. In the American clinics there were nice little notices asking people not to eat and drink in the waiting rooms in case of spillage. The contrast couldn't have been bigger if we'd found ourselves on Mars.

We finished the day with an EEG. Henry didn't try to pull the wires off; he slept when they wanted him to and stared at the strobe light on demand. They got a perfect reading. Henry's brain was showing curious patterns. Not quite what they were expecting. When Henry had last had an EEG done in England they'd told us it was 'normal'.

Jim had wanted to rule out autism as part of Henry's problems. Dr Joe Donnelly, a specialist in this condition, quickly ruled it out for Henry. We asked him also to take a look at Freddie, who was playing in the waiting room and whom we believed to be autistic. Several people, including his teachers, had told us that they believed Freddie to be autistic, but getting a diagnosis in the UK is hard. If autism is diagnosed you are potentially entitled to a lot more help. Don't diagnose it and there's no need to offer help. Our scenario exactly.

Two hours later Dr Donnelly diagnosed Freddie as autistic. He also said he had dyspraxia (spatial awareness problems) and dysarthria (slurred speech). It was a relief, after so long, to have such a clear diagnosis.

That night we collapsed and slept fitfully – it's amazing how jetlag can prevent sleep, even in extreme exhaustion

– and we all woke at some hideously early hour. We had a couple of free days before the next set of medical interviews and tests, so by 8 a.m. we were heading for Disneyland. I think if we had waited a minute longer Freddie would have expired with longing.

Disneyland was an extraordinary place. Adults became excited children again and there were numerous centres for 'lost parents'. We were lucky to be given an 'exit pass' for disabled people, which meant we bypassed the queues for the rides and got straight on. Despite our exhaustion, we all had tremendous fun. Some of the rides had the most hair-raising special effects. Freddie's favourite, though not for Henry or the faint-hearted, was the Indiana Jones ride where you were seated in a jeep that hurtled you at high speed, ducking, weaving and screeching, through incredible scenes. The highlight for Freddie was meeting Winnie the Pooh. Convinced that this adult-sized Disney version was the Winnie he had always adored, Freddie shook with nerves from head to toe and was totally over-awed when Winnie gave him a hug. We asked him whether he'd like to meet Eeyore or Tigger too, but Freddie said a loud 'No'. He had reached his limit!

The next day we headed for Sea World in San Diego. Freddie was deeply unimpressed, rides by now being absolutely paramount to him after our day at Disney. He completely ignored the spectacular killer whale show, during which these enormous creatures shot vertically out of the water, showering a joyfully screaming audience with huge amounts of water. I had covered both boys with waterproofs but a large deluge of water still hit

Henry squarely in the face and started him roaring in fury and indignation. Sea World was definitely not a hit with the boys, but for us adults the day was made when we managed to stroke dolphins.

We arrived back at our bungalow to find an email from Jim saying he had set up the SPECT scan at a private clinic for eight o'clock the next morning. My stomach lurched. This was my hour of truth. Had my instinct been right? Would the scan show something in Henry's brain function that could be treated?

The clinic was small and spotlessly clean. We were ushered into a waiting room and asked to fill out a few forms, and then a young man came and took us into a preparation room. I dreaded the fact that Henry had to be sedated and then injected with radioactive dye for this scan, but in fact it was all done very calmly and quickly. He flinched when injected – but didn't cry, much to our amazement. Maximum oral sedation was given, and after ten minutes Henry fell asleep with his head in the scanner and my fingers gently holding his chin so that his head didn't move. The machine clicked and whirred away and Henry didn't stir. My great worry was that my arm was beginning to ache horribly. The desperation to straighten it was becoming quite over-whelming, but I knew that if I moved his face one millimetre the scan could be wasted. They needed to get still clear shots, and movement of any sort would blur the reading. Somehow I managed to keep my arm in position and Henry miraculously remained asleep. The moment the technician said they'd got a perfect reading Henry came round and, rather groggily, sat up. I felt a very nice Guardian Angel had looked after us that morning.

We took Henry back to the bungalow for a rest, only to find a message from the clinic inviting us straight back to discuss the results. I felt surprisingly calm – the stomach churning had stopped. Somehow I just knew it would be OK. Back at the clinic its director sat us down and got the scans out. He explained that although Henry's brain was all there – which we knew from the MRI scans – areas of it appeared to be dormant. Why they weren't functioning he couldn't say.

Late that afternoon, armed with Henry's scans, we were sent to another top specialist. Dr Shankle was partially deaf and couldn't hear the pitch of my voice, so Michael did all the talking while Henry sat next to us in his wheelchair jigging backwards and forwards. Dr Shankle was an Alzheimer's expert. Spreading Henry's scans out on the table, he quickly ran through them. He said he could tell just from looking at the scans exactly what Henry liked seeing, such as lines. Our jaws dropped – Henry does love grids, lines and straight objects like radiators. He pointed out that Henry's vision was limited, not by his eyes, but by the messages being received in his brain, and that Henry was bound to latch on to something that he actually could see – such as lines. He also said that Henry's peripheral eyesight was excellent. We knew this was true – Henry could appear to be looking forward yet grab something off to one side.

Dr Shankle told us that Henry was operating in what is known as the Alpha state. This is a state that many people spend thousands of pounds trying to achieve. It's the deepest state of meditation and the equivalent of having an out-of-body experience. Henry was permanently in this state and apparently much to be envied. Normal human brains operate at about 60–70 Hertz, but Henry's was operating at about 7–12 Hertz. It's as if he was awake and asleep at the same time.

The lack of visible damage to Henry's brain, and the fact that he could associate it with pictures of the brains of Alzheimer sufferers, was enough for Dr Shankle to be able to draw up a positive plan of action. He highlighted the dormant parts of Henry's brain and told us that he believed these parts could be activated or 'switched on'. He then proceeded to write out a programme of medication, which he explained would target specific parts of Henry's brain. Our son would begin with one medication and others would be added, one at a time, to see how he responded. Slowly, by a process of deduction, they would work out which medications would work for Henry.

Once the medications began to kick in we would need to make another trip to the USA so that they could check his progress. With another EEG they would be able to measure how his brain was operating and see the visible improvements on the scan. By tracking the changes in his brain and matching them with his behavioural improvements they would know which area to target next. This was on the frontiers of medicine, and Dr Shankle couldn't tell us exactly which drugs would work for Henry or how long it might take. Only that he, along with others, believed it could be done, and that once we hit the right combination of drugs lift-off would be comprehensive. 'You'll know when it's working,' he assured us. After thanking him from the bottom of our hearts, we left clutching several armfuls of drugs – Henry's 'switch on' medication.

We drove back in silence. I wanted to weep, but felt that if I started I would never stop. I had spent fifteen years waiting for this moment and I didn't know how to analyse or cope with my feelings. Longing, excitement, disbelief, grief for the lost years and gratitude all churned within me.

I felt exhausted from the effort of trying to take it all in, but we were due to have dinner with Jim and so I started to prepare the boys' supper. Jane and Eva said they would finish it off and that I should get ready to go out – they could see I was tired. I'd cut the broccoli up and put it in a pan. The spag bol was in another pan – they just had to cook it. Since Freddie's operations I had become fastidious in his food preparation. I knew pretty much what he could and couldn't eat and we had managed to stave off any further operations, but the care I took to ensure this was immense and time-consuming. I always did all his cooking. Except tonight.

I'd just got my suit on and done my face, which made me feel semi-human again, when I returned to the kitchen to find Freddie choking on a piece of broccoli – one of the carers had under-cooked it. I grabbed a glass of hot water and made Freddie swallow as much as he could. From past experience I knew there was some chance of clearing the blockage with hot water – it almost seemed to ease the spasm. But this time the fluid hit the blockage and came straight back up. After half an hour it still wasn't clearing, the floor was awash with spewed up water and one of the girls was in tears. I asked Michael to call Jim, say we weren't going to make dinner and ask him where the nearest hospital was that we could take Freddie to. It looked as though surgery would be needed – the night promised to be a long one.

While Michael was getting directions Freddie took one last gulp and the blockage cleared. I hugged my boy as he clearly said, 'All gone,' then hugged the carer (having wanted to kill her ten minutes earlier), made some scrambled eggs and baked beans, foods that I knew to be safe, got changed again and headed out to dinner. The fact that we drove in circles for an hour when we knew exactly where Jim lived made me realise that, despite our apparent outward calmness, we were in fact bags of quaking nerves!

Despite all the contact we'd had by email over the past year, this was our first meeting with Jim. It was one of those moments that you want to encapsulate for ever. How do you say thank you for listening, for taking notice of us, for arranging all this and for giving my son the chance of a real life? We hugged – it was as if we were old friends.

Jim is a larger-than-life character – he looks like Pavarotti and has a heart to match. Diane, his lovely and, I suspect, long-suffering wife, welcomed us with open arms. I can't begin to say how lucky and privileged I felt to be with these two. Michael and I sat in their garden drinking wine and giddy with the prospect of what lay ahead. We couldn't have found a more brilliant or kinder man. I truly thanked God.

I asked Jim why he had become involved with us. He

sat and pondered, and this is what he said: 'I get a lot of emails – around 130 a day – from people asking for help for their loved ones. Most say that no one will ever answer their emails. Many people whose relatives are brain-injured or suffering from diseases such as Alzheimer's sound very desperate and very sad, and that saddens me deeply. So I try to answer all the queries with at least a short, but personalised response so people won't feel so alone, or give up. I usually suggest they check in again with me after six months so that I can tell them how our research is progressing. I rarely send a response to a second immediate query because, if I did, I would have no time at all to do any research or write. But in some exceptional cases – yours being one – I sense something beyond what I usually hear or read. You expressed directly and indirectly a sense of positive, enduring commitment and love that most people do not have. You seemed to embody the full, heroic sense of what being a mother is all about, a love for a child that transcends what most people can endure. I knew that depth of commitment and positive attitude would be necessary, if not sufficient, to carry out what would be required to cure your sons of their neurological deficits. There is a lot to be said for the power of love, and humour, and if all of the pioneering neurological work being done around the world has a chance of working soon, it would work for a family like yours. So that's why I answered your early emails. After that, we hit it off and became pals, and pals always write to each other!'

Jim's words touched me deeply. For so long I had been made to feel a nuisance and as though my children were worthless. Yet here was a man who was the polar opposite of all those uncaring people we had dealt with over the years. He believed in me, and he understood hope. I had asked him to look at Henry's scans and he had said yes when so many might have said no. He had taken the time to analyse them and then said, 'Good thing you stuck in there – something can be done.' He was undoing fifteen years of rejection and giving us hope. I felt very humble faced with such overwhelming, life-changing generosity. How do you express gratitude of such enormity that you cannot even begin to measure it?

On our last evening we watched the fireworks behind Sleeping Beauty's castle in Disneyland. Fairies and wishing stars flew across the sky – the crowds were invited to make wishes and told they were sure to come true if you believed enough. I looked down at Henry and knew that my wishes were finally coming true. His journey had begun.

Epilogue: Six Months Later

When Henry began his first course of medication, starting in June 2003, every emotion ran through me. I had never given Henry so much as an antibiotic before, and was filled with trepidation that the medication might do more harm than good. The drugs we were prescribed had never been used before for a disabled child, only in cases of adult dementia. This was cutting-edge stuff.

My fears were unfounded, and within a short space of time we began to see a marked improvement in Henry's vision – in fact so much so that we could now legitimately classify him as 'seeing' rather than being visually impaired with blind sight. It was as if one day he could suddenly see clearly – the images arrived in his brain and he could analyse them. The receptors, so long dulled, were beginning to respond and kick in. We had one very funny tea party when we realised this extraordinary change had occurred. A guest arrived and sat next to Henry. Our son turned his face to the newcomer and couldn't take his eyes off him. It was as if he had never seen a stranger before – which he hadn't! He stared and stared – we all laughed. We presented Henry with a mirror, and for the first time he grinned as he saw a handsome boy staring back. I think it took him quite a while to realise it was himself.

The downsides are that Henry wants a lot more stimulation and gets bored far more easily. He is at times very angry, frustrated and agitated. Though these aspects are hard to deal with, ultimately it will be this sense of frustration that will restimulate his brain.

Henry is still very disabled, but as I watch him slowly awaken there are no words to describe the pure joy I feel. I have no doubt that we are finally on the right path to unlocking him.

Three years ago Professor Ramachandran mentioned in passing that Henry's condition – blind sight – and Freddie's condition – autism – came from the same area of the brain. I stored this information. When Henry's sight dramatically improved it seemed logical that Freddie, who was now clinically diagnosed as autistic, should start on the same medication. Dr Shankle and Jim Fallon agreed that there was every possibility that the medication would also help Freddie. Out-of-the-box thinking, but it made perfect sense. We started Freddie's medication in mid-January 2004. Will it work? We can only wait and see.

Six months after completing the book I can look back and say how much it helped me to look objectively at all that I had gone through. Many people have said they would have collapsed in a heap or been left incredibly bitter by all that we have been put through. I can't say I came out unscathed – the battles were a tough call, and at times I certainly felt angry and miserable. But these emotions never dominated for any length of time, and somehow a balance has been reached and a cycle has ended. Letting go and moving on has been fundamental to our future.

My dream that both my boys will be well has never altered since that first day when I saw Henry standing tall and well in the library. I truly believe we all chose this path. It has been a tough one, but my love for my boys has kept me going. I have never doubted their healing.

The Henry Spink Foundation is an independent charity created to help families of children with severe disabilities of all kinds. We provide information on conventional and complementary/alternative medicine, therapies and research relating to a very wide range of physical and mental disorders. We gather information from practitioners, specialists, associations and centres of excellence all over the world in order to provide detailed information from our database, and all our fact-sheets are available on line. Particularly focussing on children, the Foundation also helps adults.

We are extending the activities of the Foundation to include information on the special needs education system within the UK, access to social services and the rights of disabled children and adults.

To help our research, we are gathering data and stories from those with disabled children. Direct experience of the statementing process, finding suitable schools, getting help with care at home and other practical issues will be used to assist other parents. If you would like to contribute, please email us at *stories@henryspink.org*. While the Foundation cannot respond to individual messages, we will endeavour to ensure that all information is used to improve the lives of disabled children.

The activities of the Foundation need funding, as we provide all information without charge. If you are able to support the Foundation, please contact us through the link on the website.

www.henryspink.org

If you wish to support the need for change to legislation concerning disabled people, please register your interest at *www.henriettasdream.org*

Registered Charity No: 1055469